Editor
Sara Connolly

Cover Artist
Brenda DiAntonis

Editor in Chief
Ina Massler Levin, M.A.

Creative Director
Karen J. Goldfluss, M.S. Ed.

Imaging
James Edward Grace
Craig Gunnell

Publisher
Mary D. Smith, M.S. Ed.

COMPUTER PROJECTS

Grades 5-6

Includes Standards & Benchmarks

Integrate technology into the curriculum!

- Computer lessons for Word Processing, Spreadsheets, and Presentations
- Step-by-step instructions and screenshots
- Works with a variety of software packages

Author

Steve Butz

Teacher Created Resources, Inc.
6421 Industry Way
Westminster, CA 92683
www.teachercreated.com

ISBN: 978-1-4206-2394-9

© 2010 Teacher Created Resources, Inc.
Made in U.S.A.

Teacher Created Resources

Table of Contents

Word Processing Activities

Spreadsheet Activities

Presentation Activity

Introduction

Computer Activities for Grades 5–6 is an activity book that was created to accommodate teachers who would like to utilize computer technology to enhance the curriculum. The activities in this book were designed for use in a computer lab setting for grades five and six.

The book is arranged into three sections, which correlate to the use of three different types of software applications: word processing, spreadsheets, and presentations. There are 20 activities contained in this book that address the many different ways in which elementary educators can use software. This offers teachers the opportunity to confidently take classes into the computer lab and present a well-rounded lesson using software available in their schools.

Presentation

Spreadsheet

Word Processing

Each activity is noted as it pertains to the topic of study, and everything needed to implement each lesson effectively is contained within the lab. Every activity has been successfully used in the classroom and is designed so that it can be completed in one 45-minute computer lab session. No knowledge of software applications is required to teach the activities contained in this book.

Each lab provides you with the overall purpose of the lesson, learning objectives, materials required, and detailed step by step procedures on how to successfully implement the lesson, along with informative pictures that show you exactly what to do. Although each lesson contains specific subject matter, all labs in this book can be easily adapted to fit your specific lesson plans by using your own data. The labs are designed to illustrate the many ways that computers can be used in your classroom to reinforce your specific topic of study, and may provide you with a variety of ways to incorporate technology into your curriculum.

Parts of a Circle
Activity 1

Objectives

Each student will utilize a word processing program to create a diagram that shows the following parts of a circle: circumference, radius, diameter, chord, and center.

Benchmarks for Technology Standards

Students will know the characteristics, uses, and basic features of computer software programs, including:

- opening a file
- using basic menu commands and toolbar functions
- formatting text by centering lines
- using a word processor to apply formatting to text

Learning Objectives

At the end of this lesson, students will be able to:

1. Center, make bold, and underline the heading of a word processing document.
2. Draw a circle using the shapes tool.
3. Change the fill and line color of a shape.
4. Use the Line tool to draw lines in a document.
5. Use the Text Box tool to label each part of the circle.
6. Use the Arrow tool to connect a label to an object within a document.

Before the Computer

This activity can be completed using most versions of Microsoft Word, Open Office, and iWorks.

Variations

Depending on the grade level and time allotted for this activity, you may choose to have your students label points on the circle to define the parts. For example, the radius could be labeled Points AB, etc. Also, if time and ability levels allow, you may then choose to also draw and label a segment, sector, and semicircle. An example of a completed project is shown in Figure 1-1.

Parts of a Circle *(cont.)*
Activity 1

Parts of a Circle

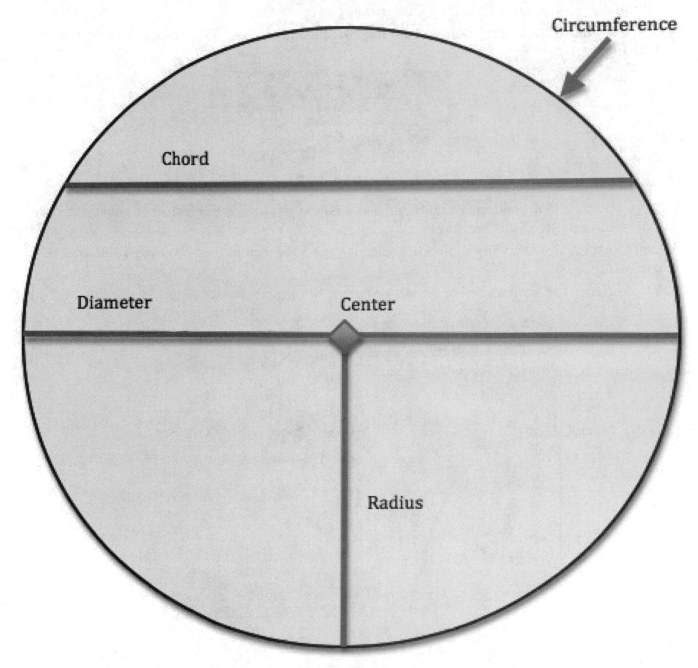

Figure 1-1

Parts of a Circle *(cont.)*
Activity 1

Procedure

1. Open a new word processing document.

2. Type the heading "Parts of a Circle" at the top of the page.

3. Highlight the heading by clicking and dragging over it.

4. Click on the **Align Center** button from the **Formatting** toolbar. This should center your heading (see Figure 1-2).

Figure 1-2

5. Now click the **Bold** button (B) and **Underline** button (U) on the **Formatting** toolbar. This will bold and underline your heading.

6. Next, display the **Drawing** toolbar by selecting the **View** menu, then choosing **Toolbars** and **Drawing**.

7. On the **Drawing** toolbar, select the **AutoShapes**, **Shapes**, or **Basic Shapes** button (Figure 1-3).

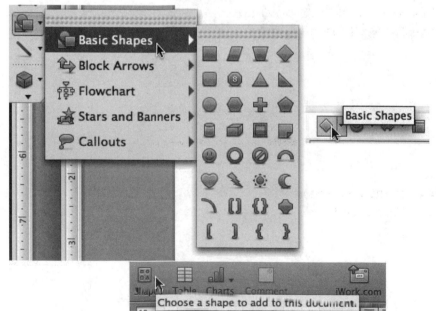

Figure 1-3

Parts of a Circle (cont.)
Activity 1

8. Now click the **Circle** icon and drag your cursor to the top-left portion of your document. Hold down the **shift** key as you click and drag to draw your circle. (Holding down the shift key will ensure that your shape is a circle and not an oval.) Make sure that your shape is not too big (Figure 1-4).

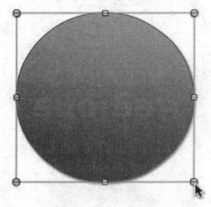

Figure 1-4

9. Now that you have drawn your circle, you will change its fill and line color. If you are using Microsoft Word, double-click on the circle to bring up the **Format AutoShapes** window. Change the **Fill** color for your circle. Choose a light shade so your circle is not too dark. Next, change the **Line** color and click **OK**.

10. Now you will use the **Line** tool to draw the diameter of your circle. To do this, click on your **Line** tool icon and select **Line** (Figure 1-5).

Figure 1-5

11. Drag your cursor to the middle-left side of your circle, and then click and draw a line from one side to the other (Figure 1-6).

Figure 1-6

Parts of a Circle *(cont.)*
Activity 1

12. Next, select the **Text Box** tool (Figure 1-7).

Figure 1-7

13. Click and drag your cursor above your line near the left part of the circle, and type the label "Diameter" in your text box (Figure 1-8).

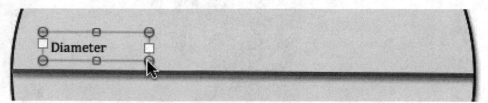

Figure 1-8

14. Next, use your **Line** tool to draw a line from the center of your circle down to the edge to represent the radius (Figure 1-9).

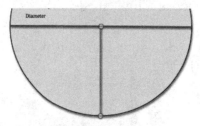

Figure 1-9

15. Now use the **Text Box** tool to label the radius.

16. Next, select the **AutoShapes** or **Shapes** tool and choose the **Diamond**. Click and drag your cursor to draw a small diamond shape at the center of the circle. Use the **Text Box** tool to label the center (Figure 1-10).

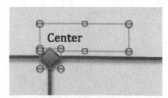

Figure 1-10

17. Use the **Text Box** tool to draw a label near the upper right hand corner, outside of your circle. The label should read "Circumference."

Parts of a Circle *(cont.)*
Activity 1

18. Use the **Arrow** tool to draw an arrow from your circumference label to the edge of your circle (Figure 1-11).

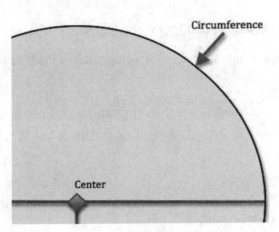

Figure 1-11

19. Use the **Line** tool to draw a line connecting the circumference across the top third of your circle (Figure 1-12).

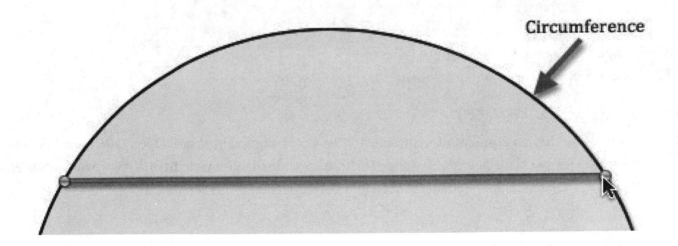

Figure 1-12

20. Finally, use the **Text Box** tool to label the line "Chord."

21. Your circle diagram is now complete.

Landscape Regions of the USA
Activity 2

Objectives

Each student will utilize a word processing program to create and label a map of the United States using the abbreviations for each state.

Benchmarks for Technology Standards

Students will know the characteristics, uses, and basic features of computer software programs including:

- the common features and uses of desktop publishing and word processing software
- knowing that documents can be created, designed, and formatted
- importing images into a document

Learning Objectives

At the end of this lesson, students will be able to:

1. Navigate to a website to access free, downloadable images.
2. Change the page layout for a document.
3. Import an image into a document.
4. Format an imported image.
5. Label an image using the Text Box tool.
6. Change the format of text within a text box.
7. Cite a reference for an image downloaded from a website.

Before the Computer

- This activity can be completed using most versions of Microsoft Word, Open Office, and iWorks.
- The following website is a great source for free, downloadable maps: **http://www.worldatlas.com** (Check to make sure the website is available before teaching this lesson.)

Variations

Depending on the grade level and time allotted for this activity, you may choose to have your students label their maps with the names or abbreviations of each state. Also, if you have more experienced students and more time, they may be able to change the state labels' font and color. An example of a completed project is shown in Figure 2-1.

Landscape Regions of the USA *(cont.)*
Activity 2

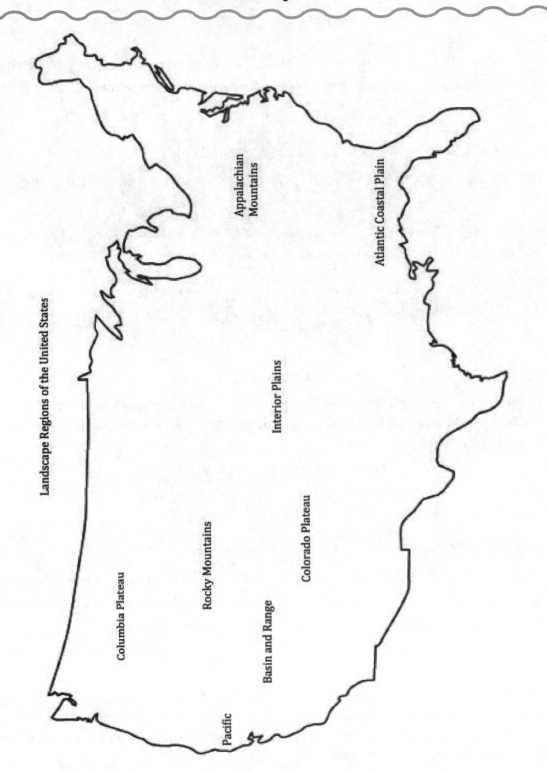

Landscape Regions of the United States

Appalachian Mountains

Atlantic Coastal Plain

Interior Plains

Columbia Plateau

Rocky Mountains

Basin and Range

Colorado Plateau

Pacific

Figure 2-1

Landscape Regions of the USA (cont.)
Activity 2

1. Open a new word processing document.

2. If you are using Microsoft Word or Open Office, open the **View** menu and select **Print View**.

3. From the **File** menu, select **Page Setup** and choose landscape orientation (Figure 2-2).

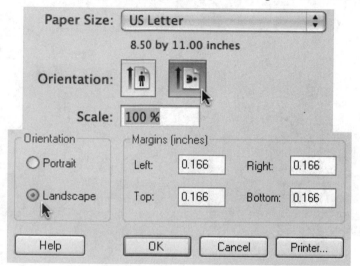

Figure 2-2

4. Type in the following title at the top of your page: "Landscape Regions of the United States." Click and drag over the title to highlight it, and use the **Align Center** button to center your title (Figure 2-3).

Figure 2-3

5. Next, using your web browser, navigate to the following website: **http://www.worldatlas.com**. Enter the website, scroll down, and click on the link on the right side that is labeled **Outline Maps**.

6. From the list choose the map USA (**continental shape only**).

7. Right-click on the map (or control-click if you are using a Mac) and choose **Copy**.

8. Return to your word processing document, and choose **Paste** from the **Edit** menu. The map should now be part of your document.

Landscape Regions of the USA (cont.)
Activity 2

9. Now you will re-size your map so its fills the entire page. Go to the **View** menu and choose **Zoom**. Reduce the size of the display of your document to **75%**. You can also change the viewing size by using the **Zoom** tool on your toolbar (Figure 2-4).

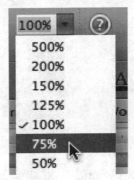

Figure 2-4

10. Next, click on your map once to show the image's anchor points. Click and drag the bottom-right corner of your map so it fills the entire page (Figure 2-5).

Figure 2-5

11. Right-click (or control-click) on the map, choose **Text Wrapping**, and **Behind Text**. This will allow you to type labels on top of your map. If you are using Open Office, choose **Wrap** and **No Wrap**. Use the **Zoom** tool to return your page to **100%** view.

12. If your drawing toolbar is not showing, select the **View** menu, choose **Toolbars**, and then select **Drawing**.

13. Select the **Text Box** tool (Figure 2-6).

Figure 2-6

Landscape Regions of the USA (cont.)
Activity 2

14. Click and drag the **Text Box** tool just above Florida to make a large box (Figure 2-7).

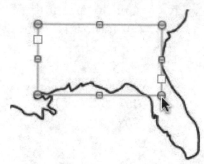

Figure 2-7

15. Click inside of the text box you just drew and type the label "Atlantic Coastal Plain."

16. If you need to enlarge the text box to make the label fit, or move the text box, click on the box and then click and drag one of the anchor points on the corners to make it smaller or larger.

17. You can also move the text box by clicking on a line and dragging the entire box to a new location. If you highlight the text within a text box, you can also change the alignment and formatting of the text (font type, size, style, color, etc.).

18. You can also change the line and fill color for your text box by right-clicking (or control-clicking) on it and choosing **Format Text Box**, and **Colors and Lines**.

19. Continue labeling your map with the names of each landscape region as shown in Figure 2-8.

Figure 2-8

20. Once you have finished labeling your map, insert a text box near the lower-right side with the following reference: "Map Source: Worldatlas.com." Your map is now complete!

14

Ecosystem Diagram
Activity 3

Objectives

Each student will utilize a word processing program to create and label a diagram of a simple ecosystem, community, and population.

Benchmarks for Technology Standards

Students will know the characteristics, uses, and basic features of computer software programs, including:

- the common features and uses of desktop publishing and word processing software
- knowing that documents can be created, designed, and formatted
- importing images into a document

Learning Objectives

At the end of this lesson, students will be able to:

1. Change the page layout for a document.
2. Center, bold, and increase font size.
3. Import and format an image into a document.
4. Label an image using the Text Box tool.
5. Draw geometric shapes using the Shapes tool.
6. Copy, paste, and resize an image within a document.
7. Use the select all command.
8. Cite a reference for an image downloaded from a website.

Before the Computer

- This activity can be completed using most versions of Microsoft Word, Open Office and iWorks.
- The following websites are a great source for free, downloadable clip art images: **http://office.microsoft.com/en-us/clipart** or **http://classroomclipart.com**
- If you use or know of other free clipart websites that are available online, they may be used with this activity as well. Check to make sure the website you choose to use for this activity is available, and you are able to copy and paste the clip art they contain into a document before teaching this lesson. Also, if you choose to use the Microsoft website, instruct your students to filter their searches only for clip art. This can be done by clicking the arrow on the **Search** button, and choosing **Clip art**.

Variations

Depending on the grade level and time allotted for this activity, you may choose to have your students add other organisms to their ecosystem, and also label each organism as a producer or consumer. They might also be able to add the non-living components of an ecosystem, like water, sunlight, clouds, etc. An example of a completed project is shown in Figure 3-1.

Ecosystem Diagram (cont.)
Activity 3

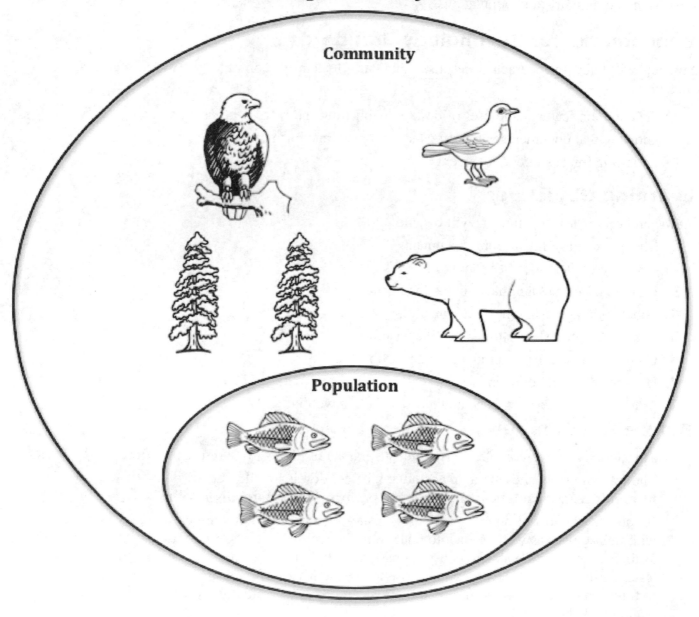

A Simple Ecosystem

Community

Population

Figure 3-1

Ecosystem Diagram *(cont.)*
Activity 3

Procedure

1. Open a new word processing document.

2. If you are using Microsoft Word or Open Office, open the **View** menu and select **Print View**.

3. From the **File** menu, select **Page Setup**, and choose landscape orientation (Figure 3-2). If you are using **Open Office**, choose the **Format** menu, and **Page**.

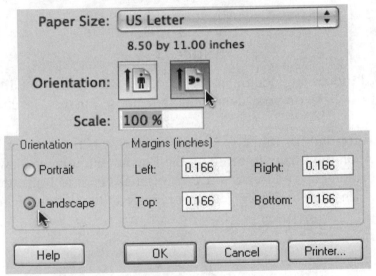

Figure 3-2

4. Next, type in the following title: "A Simple Ecosystem."

5. Highlight your title by clicking and dragging over it. Then increase its font size to 24 by clicking the **Font Size** button.

6. While your title is still highlighted, make it bold and underlined by using the **Bold** and **Underline** buttons (Figure 3-3). You may also try to make it bold and underline it by holding down the **control** key while pressing either the **B** key for bold or **U** key for underline. (If you are using a Mac, you must hold down the **command** key.) While you still have the title highlighted, click on the **Align Center** button to center your title.

7. Next, open up your web browser and navigate to one of the websites below, or another site that your teacher has chosen.

http://office.microsoft.com/en-us/clipart or **http://classroomclipart.com**

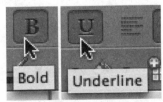

Figure 3-3

Ecosystem Diagram *(cont.)*
Activity 3

8. These websites hold many free, downloadable images that can be imported into your word processing document. You are going to use one of them to access images of organisms that will make up your ecosystem. In the search box on the webpage, choose **Clipart** from the drop-down menu, and type in the word "Trout." Your search will reveal many different images of trout. Locate one you like, and click on the copy icon below the image (Figure 3-4), or right-click on your mouse (control-click on a Mac) and choose **Copy Image**.

Figure 3-4

9. Return to your word processing document and choose **Paste** from the **Edit** menu. You can also right-click (or control-click) on your document and choose **Paste**. The image should now be part of your document.

10. Next, you'll need to format the image so you can place it where you want in the document. To do this, double-click on the image to bring up the **Format Picture** window. Choose **Layout**, and **Behind Text**, or you can right-click (or control-click) on it to bring up the **Format Picture** window. Then you can click and drag your trout image to the bottom center of your page.

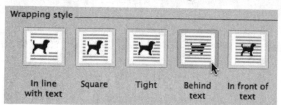

Figure 3-5

11. Now, make sure your trout image is highlighted. To highlight an image, click on it once to reveal its anchor points. You can re-size the image by clicking and dragging on one of the anchor points to make it larger or smaller. Once your image is highlighted, right-click on it and choose **Copy**. Right-click (or control-click) on your page just to the right of the trout image and choose **Paste**. A copy of your trout should appear. Repeat this two more times to make a total of four trout (Figure 3-6).

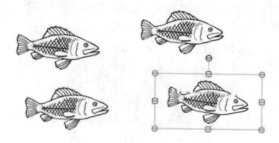

Figure 3-6

Ecosystem Diagram *(cont.)*
Activity 3

12 Now click on the **Drawing** toolbar, and select the **AutoShapes**, **Shapes**, or **Basic Shapes** button (Figure 3-7).

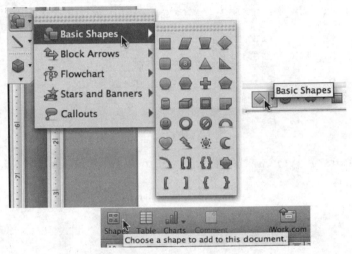

Figure 3-7

13. Now, click the **Circle** icon and click and drag it to make a circle over your four fish. Right-click (or control-click) on the circle, choose **Format Auto Shape**, select **Colors and Lines**, and under **Fi**ll, select **No Fill**.

14. The four trout represent a group of the same species of organisms, also known as a *population*. Select your **Text Box** tool and click and drag it over the top portion of your circle to form a box. Type the following label into the text box: "Population." Next, highlight the label, center it using the **Align Center** button, and increase its font size to **14** (Figure 3-8).

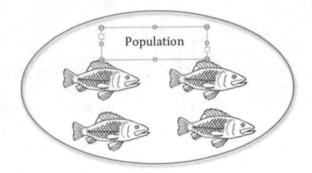

Figure 3-8

15. Next, return to the clipart website and search for an image of a bear. Copy and paste it into your page above the four trout. Make sure to format the picture so it sits behind the text. Also, search for, copy, and paste the following images above the bear: **Eagle**, **Robin**, and **Tree** (Figure 3-9).

16. Use the shapes tool again to draw a circle around all of your organisms, including your trout. Make sure to change the fill to **No Fill**.

Ecosystem Diagram *(cont.)*
Activity 3

17. All of the living things within an ecosystem are called a *community*. Select the **Text Box** tool to label all of the organisms within the circle as a "Community."

18. If you want to move all of the images in your document, select the **Select Objects** tool.

Figure 3-9

19. Click and drag your cursor over all of the images in your diagram to highlight them (Figure 3-10).

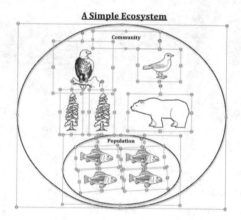

Figure 3-10

20. Now you can move all of your images at once by clicking and dragging them with your mouse to relocate them if necessary.

21. Next, use the **Text Box** tool to cite the website you used for your clipart. Select the **Text Box** tool, and click and drag it to make a box near the lower right part of your diagram. Type in the web page source that you used for your images into the text box (Figure 3-11).

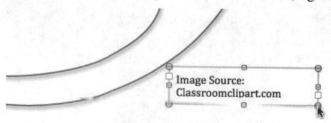

Figure 3-11

22. Your project is now complete!

Technology Time Line
Activity 4

Objectives

Each student will utilize a word processing program to create and label a flowchart representing the different periods of technological development.

Benchmarks for Technology Standards

Students will know the characteristics, uses, and basic features of computer software programs, including:

- the common features and uses of desktop publishing and word processing software
- knowing that documents can be created, designed, and formatted

Learning Objectives

At the end of this lesson, students will be able to:

1. Change the page layout for a document.
2. Center, make bold, and increase font size.
3. Use the Block Arrows tool to make a time line.
4. Change the fill color within a block arrow.
5. Usc the Text Box tool to create labels.
6. Change the font size within a text box.
7. Change the alignment of text within a text box.

Before the Computer

This activity can be completed using most versions of Microsoft Word, Open Office, and iWorks.

Variations

Depending on the grade level and time allotted for this activity, you may choose to have your students add more information about inventions or the development of tools and processes to each historical period that makes up the timeline. An example of a completed project is shown in Figure 4-1.

Technology Time Line *(cont.)*
Activity 4

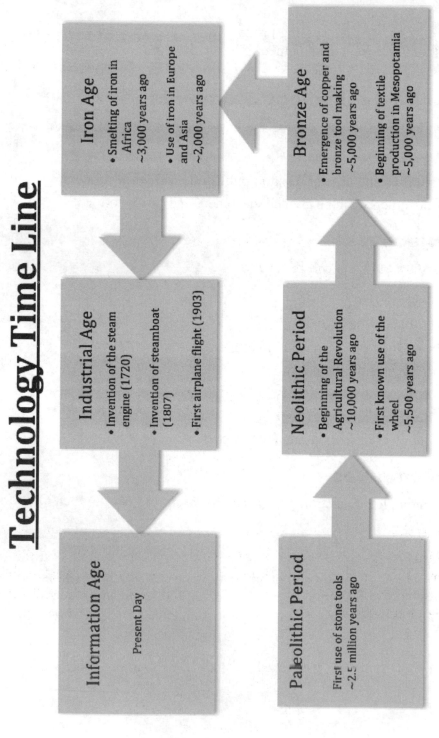

Technology Time Line

Iron Age
- Smelting of iron in Africa ~3,000 years ago
- Use of iron in Europe and Asia ~2,000 years ago

Bronze Age
- Emergence of copper and bronze tool making ~5,000 years ago
- Beginning of textile production in Mesopotamia ~5,000 years ago

Industrial Age
- Invention of the steam engine (1720)
- Invention of steamboat (1807)
- First airplane flight (1903)

Neolithic Period
- Beginning of the Agricultural Revolution ~10,000 years ago
- First known use of the wheel ~5,500 years ago

Information Age

Present Day

Paleolithic Period

First use of stone tools ~2.5 million years ago

Figure 4-1

22

Technology Time Line (cont.)
Activity 4

Procedure

1. Open a new word processing document.

2. If you are using Microsoft Word or Open Office, open the **View** menu and select **Print View**.

3. From the **File** menu, select **Page Setup,** and choose **Landscape** orientation (Figure 4-2).

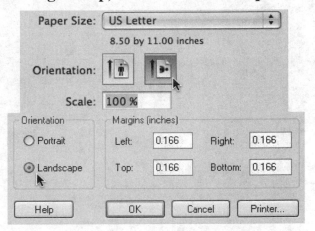

Figure 4-2

4. Type in the following title at the top of your page: "Technology Time Line." Click and drag over the title to highlight it, and use the **Align Center** button to center your title (Figure 4-3).

Figure 4-3

5. While your title is still highlighted, increase its font size to **36** by clicking the **Font Size** button.

6. With your title still highlighted, make it bold and underlined by using the **Bold** and **Underline** buttons (Figure 4-4). You can also make it bold and underline it by holding down the **control** key while hitting either the **B** key for bold or **U** key for underline. If you are using a Mac, you must hold down the **command** key.

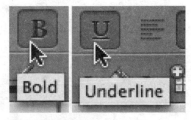

Figure 4-4

Technology Time Line *(cont.)*
Activity 4

7. Next, click **AutoShapes**, choose the **Block Arrows** tool, and select the **Right Arrow Callout** shape (Figure 4-5)

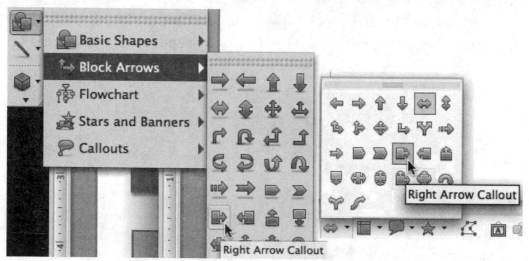

Figure 4-5

8. Click and drag your cursor to draw a block arrow in the lower-left part of your page (Figure 4-6).

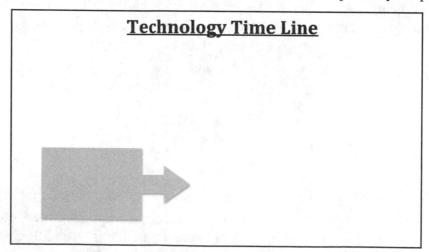

Figure 4-6

9. Right-click (or control-click) on the shape and choose **Format Autoshape**, select **Colors and Lines**, and then you can change the fill color and line color for your block arrow. If you are using Open Office, right-click (or control-click) and choose **Area**. Select a light gray for a fill color, then select **Line** to change the line color.

10. Next, select the **Text Box** tool, and click and drag it within the top portion of your block arrow box. Type in the following label: "Paleolithic Period."

11. Highlight the text in the text box and increase its font size to **18**. With your text still highlighted, use the **Align Center** button.

Technology Time Line (cont.)
Activity 4

12. Now, draw a new text box near the middle of your block arrow box and type the following information: "First Use of Stone Tools ~ 2.5 million years ago." The first part of your time line should appear like the one in Figure 4-7.

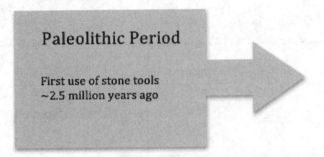

Figure 4-7

13. Use the **Block Arrow** and **Basic Shapes** tools to draw five more boxes to represent the remaining technological time periods. Use Figure 4-8 to help you draw the different boxes to make up the rest of your timeline. Make sure to change the fill color to a light gray for each box.

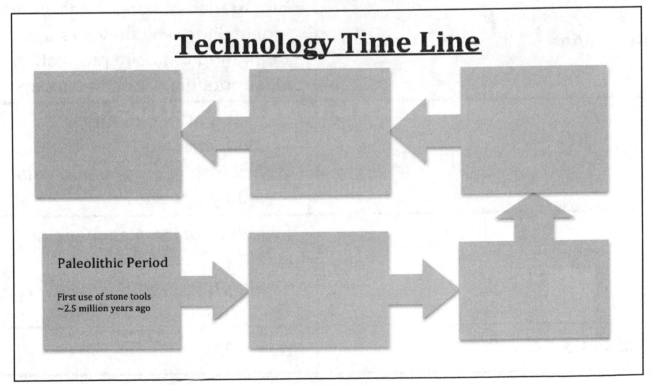

Figure 4-8

Technology Time Line (cont.)
Activity 4

14. Now you can fill in the information for the name and information for each period. Use the data table below to help you build your timeline.

Period	Information
Paleolithic	First use of stone tools ~ 2.5 million years ago
Neolithic	• Beginning of the Agricultural Revolution ~ 10,000 years ago • First known use of the wheel ~ 5,500 years ago
Bronze Age	• Emergence of copper and bronze tool making ~ 5,000 years ago • Beginning of textile production in Mesopotamia ~ 5,000 years ago
Iron Age	• Smelting of iron in Africa ~ 3,000 years ago • Use of iron in Europe and Asia ~ 2,000 years ago
Industrial Age	• Invention of the steam engine (1720) • Invention of steamboat (1807) • First airplane flight (1903)
Information Age	Present Day

15. Your technology timeline is now complete!

Exponential Notation Table
Activity 5

Objectives

Each student will create a table in a word processing document to use for learning to read and write numbers in standard form, word form, and exponential form up to the trillions.

Benchmarks for Technology Standards

Students will know the characteristics, uses, and basic features of computer software programs, including:

- the common features and uses of desktop publishing and word processing software
- knowing that documents can be created, designed, and formatted
- using a word processor to print text

Learning Objectives

At the end of this lesson, students will be able to:

1. Create a new word processing document.
2. Design and insert tables into a document.
3. Format a table.
4. Format the fill color of cells in a table.
5. Enter text into a table.
6. Format text within a table.
7. Use the superscript function to format numbers.

Before the Computer

This activity can be completed using most versions of Microsoft Word, Open Office, and iWorks.

Variations

Depending on the grade level and topic of study, you may choose to have students create a table that contains different examples of exponential numbers. An example of a completed document is shown in Figure 5-1.

Exponential Notation Table (cont.)
Activity 5

Exponential Numbers

Number Form	Tens	Hundreds	Thousands	Ten Thousands	Hundred Thousands
Standard	10	100	1,000	10,000	100,000
Word	ten	one hundred	one thousand	ten thousand	one hundred thousand
Exponential	10^1	10^2	10^3	10^4	10^5

Number Form	Millions	Ten Millions	One Hundred Millions	Billions	Ten Billions	One Hundred Billions
Standard	1,000,000	10,000,000	100,000,000	1,000,000,000	10,000,000,000	100,000,000,000
Word	one million	ten million	one hundred million	one billion	ten billions	one hundred billion
Exponential	10^6	10^7	10^8	10^9	10^{10}	10^{11}

Number Form	Trillions	Ten Trillions	One Hundred Trillions
Standard	1,000,000,000,000	10,000,000,000,000	100,000,000,000,000
Word	one trillion	ten trillion	one hundred trillion
Exponential	10^{12}	10^{13}	10^{14}

Figure 5-1

Exponential Notation Table (cont.)
Activity 5

Procedure

1. Open a new word processing document.

2. From the **File** menu, select **Page Setup**, and choose **Landscape** orientation

3. Type in the following title: "Exponential Numbers."

4. Highlight the title by clicking and dragging over it. Then center it by clicking on the **Align Center** icon (Figure 5-2). Your title should now be centered.

Figure 5-2

5. Increase the font size of your title by choosing the **Font Size** button and selecting **24** (Figure 5-3).

Figure 5-3

6. Select **Underline** and **Bold** buttons while your title is still highlighted (Figure 5-4).

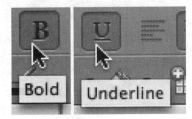

Figure 5-4

7. Hit the **enter** key twice to move down two lines. Take off the **Bold**, **Underline** format, and reduce the font size to **12**.

8. From the **Table** menu, choose **Insert** and **Table**. If you are using iWorks, click on the table icon.

9. In the **Insert Table** window, enter **6** for the number of columns, and **4** for the number of rows. Click **OK**.

Exponential Notation Table (cont.)
Activity 5

10. Next, enter the following headings in the top cells of your table: **Number Form**, **Tens**, **Hundreds**, **Thousands**, **Ten Thousands**, **Hundred Thousands** (Figure 5-5).

Exponential Numbers Table

Number Form	Tens	Hundreds	Thousands	Ten Thousands	Hundred Thousands

Figure 5-5

11. Highlight your column headings in the first row of the table by clicking and dragging over them.

12. Click on the **Align Center** button to center your headings, then make them bold.

13. Now fill in the following number forms into the first column: "Standard," "Word," and "Exponential" (Figure 5-6). Highlight the three labels and italicize them by using the **Italics** button (*I*).

Number Form	**Tens**	**Hundreds**
Standard		
Word		
Exponential		

Figure 5-6

14. Next, you will change the shade of the headings within your table. To do this, highlight the headings and choose the **Cell Background Fill** tool from the **Table** toolbar. If your **Table** toolbar is not showing, go to the **View** menu, choose **Toolbars**, and select **Tables** and **Borders**. Choose a light gray color using the **Shading Color** button (Figure 5-7).

Figure 5-7

15. Now you are ready to fill in the different forms of numbers up to the hundreds of thousands place within your table. To enter the exponential form of ten, type in "101" into the cell next to Exponential, highlight the "1" in the ones place, select the **Format** menu, **Font**, and put a check mark next to **Superscript**. See Figure 5-8 as an example of how your table should appear.

Number Form	Tens	Hundreds	Thousands	Ten Thousands	Hundred Thousands
Standard	10	100	1,000		
Word	ten	one hundred	one thousand		
Exponential	10^1	10^2	10^3		

Figure 5-8

Exponential Notation Table (cont.)
Activity 5

16. After you complete your table, click below it, hit the **enter** key on your keyboard once and insert a new table into your document. Set up the table with four rows and six columns.

17. Next, enter the following headings in the top cells of your table: "Number Form," "Millions," "Ten Millions," "One Hundred Millions," "Billions," "Ten Billions," "One Hundred Billions" (Figure 5-9).

Number Form	Millions	Ten Millions	One Hundred Millions	Billions	Ten Billions	One Hundred Billions

Figure 5-9

18. Highlight your column headings in the first row, then use the **Align Center** button to center your headings, and also make them bold.

19. Now fill in the following number forms into the first column: "Standard," "Word," and "Exponential." Highlight the three labels and italicize them using the **Italics** button (I).

20. Change the shade of the headings within your table to a light gray color.

21. Now you are ready to fill in the different forms of numbers up to hundreds of trillions place within your table. Use the **Superscript** font format option for your exponents. See Figure 5-10 as an example of how your table should appear.

Number Form	Millions	Ten Millions	One Hundred Millions	Billions	Ten Billions	One Hundred Billions
Standard	1,000,000	10,000,000	100,000,000			
Word	one million	ten million	one hundred million			
Exponential	10^6	10^7	10^8			

Figure 5-10

22. After you have completely filled in all of the information for your second table, click below it, and press the **shift + enter** keys on your keyboard to add a page break and create a new page. Then you can insert a third new table into your document. Set up the table with four rows and five columns.

23. Next, set your font size to **14** and then enter the following headings in the top cells of your table: "**Number Form, Trillions, Ten Trillions, One Hundred Trillions.**"

24. Format your table exactly as you did for the first two tables, and enter all of the information. If you wish to, you can center all the information in your table.

25. Your project is now complete!

Ancient Civilizations Map
Activity 6

Objectives

Each student will utilize a word processing program to create and label a map of the world illustrating the locations of the nine ancient civilizations including Mesopotamia, China, Egypt, India (Indus Valley), Greece, Rome, Aztec, Maya, and Inca, along with the continents in which they were located.

Benchmarks for Technology Standards

Students will know the characteristics, uses, and basic features of computer software programs, including:

- the common features and uses of desktop publishing and word processing software
- knowing that documents can be created, designed, and formatted
- importing images into a document

Learning Objectives

At the end of this lesson, students will be able to:

1. Navigate to a website to access free, downloadable images.
2. Change the page layout for a document.
3. Import an image into a document.
4. Format an imported image.
5. Change the transparency of an image.
6. Label an image using the Text Box tool.
7. Change the format of text within a text box.
8. Insert a header into a document
9. Cite a reference for an image downloaded from a website.

Before the Computer

- This activity can be completed using most versions of Microsoft Word, Open Office, and iWorks.
- The following website is a great source for free, downloadable maps:
  http://www.worldatlas.com
  Check to make sure the website is available before teaching this lesson.

Variations

Depending on the grade level and time allotted for this activity, you may choose to have your students label their map with the names of rivers or other bodies of water where these ancient civilizations began, or any other ancient civilizations you are studying. An example of a completed project is shown in Figure 6-7.

Ancient Civilizations Map *(cont.)*
Activity 6

Procedure

1. Open a new word processing document.

2. If you are using Microsoft Word or Open Office, open the **View** menu and select **Print View**.

3. From the **File** menu, select **Page Setup**, and choose **Landscape** orientation (Figure 6-1).

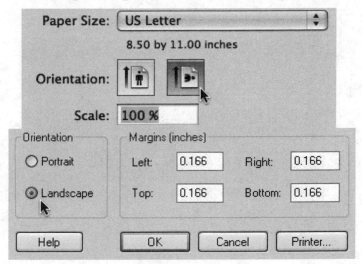

Figure 6-1

4. Next, using your web browser, navigate to the following website: **http://www.worldatlas.com**. Enter the website, scroll down, and click on the link on the right side labeled **Outline Maps**.

5. From the list choose the **World (continent borders only)** map.

6. Right-click (or control-click) on the map and choose **Copy**.

7. Return to your word processing document and choose **Paste** from the **Edit** menu. The map should now be part of your document. You can also right-click (or control-click) on your page and select **Paste**.

8. Now you will re-size your map so its fills the entire page. Go to the **View** menu, and choose **Zoom**. Reduce the size of the display of your document to **75%**. You can also change the viewing size by using the **Zoom** tool on your toolbar (Figure 6-2).

Figure 6-2

Ancient Civilizations Map *(cont.)*
Activity 6

9. Right-click (or control-click) on the map, choose **Text Wrapping**, and select **Behind Text.** This will allow you to type labels on top of your map. If you are using Open Office, choose **Wrap** and **No Wrap.**

10. Next, click on your map once to show the image's anchor points. Click and drag the bottom right corner of your map so it fills the entire page (Figure 6-3).

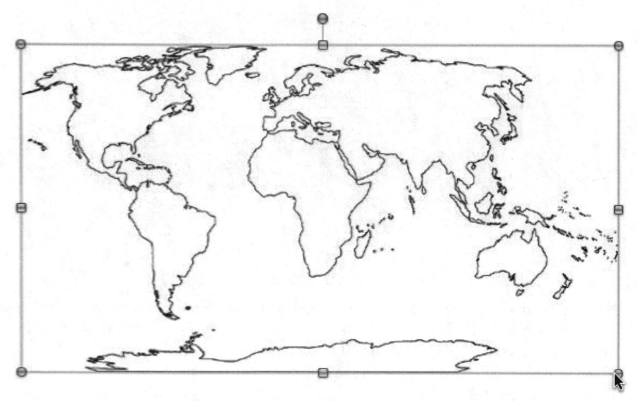

Figure 6-3

11. Use the **Zoom** tool to return your page to 100% view.

12. Next you are going to insert a header into your document, where you will type in your map's title. Open the **View** menu and select **Header and Footer**, or, if you are using Open Office, choose the **Insert** menu and select **Header**. Type the following title into your header: **Ancient Civilizations**. Click and drag over the title to highlight it and use the **Align Center** button to center it (Figure 6-4).

Figure 6-4

Ancient Civilizations Map *(cont.)*
Activity 6

13. Next, you are going to change the transparency of your map image. The transparency makes your image lighter and therefore easier to label. Right-click (or control-click) on your map image, select **Format Picture**, choose **Picture**, and set the transparency to **50%**. Click **OK**.

14. If your drawing toolbar is not showing, select the **View** menu, choose **Toolbars**, then **Drawing**.

15. Select the **Text Box** tool (Figure 6-5).

Figure 6-5

16. Click and drag the **Text Box** tool over the Middle East to make a large box and type in the label "Mesopotamia" (Figure 6-6).

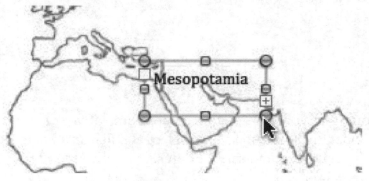

Figure 6-6

17. If you need to enlarge the text box to make the label fit or move the text box, click on the box and then click and drag one of the anchor points on the corners to make it smaller or larger.

18. You can also move the text box by clicking on a line and dragging the entire box to a new location. If you highlight the text within a text box, you can also change the alignment and formatting of the text (font type, size, style, color, alignment, etc.).

Ancient Civilizations Map *(cont.)*
Activity 6

19. Continue labeling your map with the names of each ancient civilization as shown in Figure 6-7.

Figure 6-7

20. Finally, insert a footer that you will use to cite the source of your map ("Map Source: worldatlas.com"). Open the **View** menu and select **Header and Footer**, or, if you are using Open Office, choose the **Insert** menu and select **Footer**.

21. Your project is now complete!

Simple Machines Diagram
Activity 7

Objectives

Each student will utilize a word processing program to create a diagram that shows the following seven simple machines: wedge, lever, inclined plane, gear, wheel and axle, screw, and pulley.

Benchmarks for Technology Standards

Students will know the characteristics, uses, and basic features of computer software programs including:

- opening a file
- using basic menu commands and toolbar functions
- formatting text by centering lines
- using a word processor to apply formatting to text

Learning Objectives

At the end of this lesson, students will be able to:

1. Center, bold, and underline the heading of a word processing document.
2. Draw seven basic simple machines using the Shapes tool.
3. Change the fill and line color of a shape.
4. Use the Text Box tool to label each figure.
5. Use the Rotate tool.
6. Apply the 3-D tool to a geometric shape.
7. Change the font size and alignment within a text box.

Before the Computer

This activity can be completed using most versions of Microsoft Word, Open Office, and iWorks.

Variations

Depending on the grade level and time allotted for this activity, you may choose to have your students add a short description of each simple machine or an example of a tool that utilizes a simple machine. An example of a completed project is shown in Figure 7-1.

Simple Machines Diagram (cont.)
Activity 7

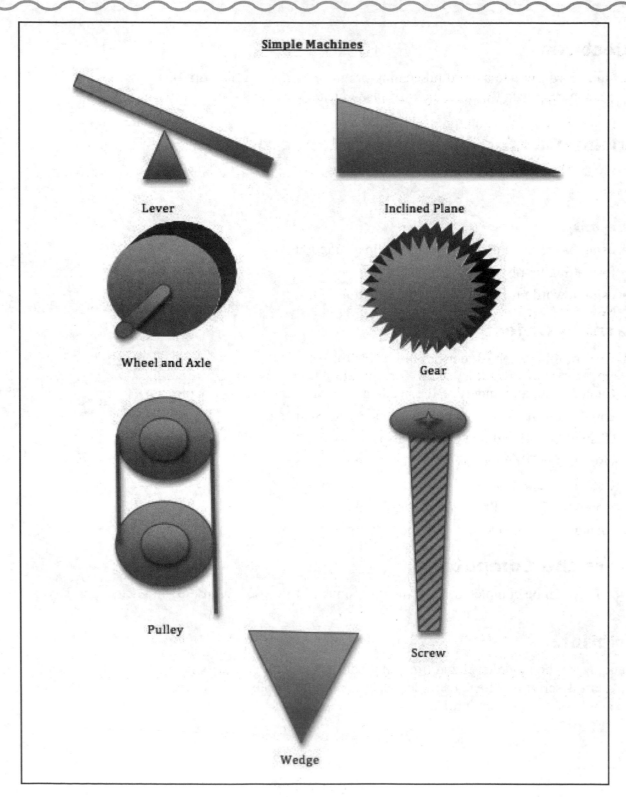

Figure 7-1

Simple Machines Diagram *(cont.)*
Activity 7

Procedure

1. Open a new word processing document.
2. Type the following heading at the top of the page: "Simple Machines."
3. Highlight your heading by clicking and dragging over it.
4. Click on the **Align Center** button from the formatting toolbar. This should center your heading (see Figure 7-2).

Figure 7-2

5. Now click the **Bold** button (B) and **Underline** button (U) on the formatting toolbar. This will make your headline bold and underline it.
6. Next, display the **Drawing** toolbar by selecting the **View** menu, **Toolbars**, and **Drawing**.

   On the **Drawing** toolbar, select the **Autoshapes**, **Shapes**, or **Basic Shapes** button (Figure 7-3).

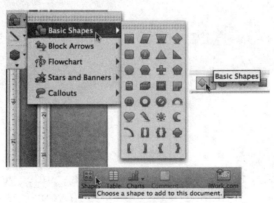

Figure 7-3

7. The first simple machine you are going to draw is a lever. A simple lever looks like a seesaw, so you are going to use the rectangle and triangle shapes tools to draw one. First, click the **square** icon, drag your cursor to the top-left portion of your document, and click and drag to draw a long, narrow rectangle about three inches long (Figure 7-4).

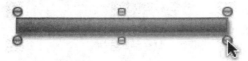

Figure 7-4

Simple Machines Diagram *(cont.)*
Activity 7

8. Next, you will need to add a triangle to act as a lever. Click the **triangle shape** tool and use it to draw a triangle directly under the rectangle you drew (Figure 7-5).

Figure 7-5

9. Now click on the rectangle you drew to highlight it, then click on the **Free Rotate** tool located on the **Drawing** toolbar (Figure 7-6).

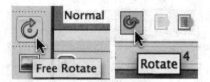

Figure 7-6

10. Click on one of the anchor points on your rectangle, drag it down so it rotates and makes your drawing look like a see-saw (Figure 7-7).

Figure 7-7

11. Now use the **Text Box** tool (Figure 7-8) to click and drag under your first simple machine and type the label "Lever." You can highlight the text within your text box and change the font type, size, style, and alignment within the text box.

Figure 7-8

Simple Machines Diagram (cont.)
Activity 7

12. Now you will draw an inclined plane. Choose the **Right Triangle** shape from the **AutoShapes** tool. Click and drag just to the right of your lever to draw a shallow triangle to represent an inclined plane (Figure 7-9).

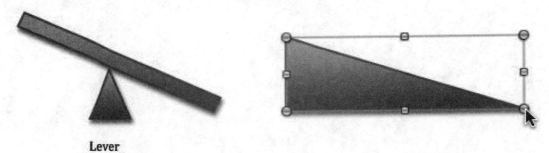

Lever

Figure 7-9

13. To change the fill or line color of your inclined plane, double-click on your shape, select **Colors and Lines**, and then select a new color for each.

14. Use the **Text Box** tool to label your inclined plane.

15. Now you will draw a wheel and axle. Choose the **Circle** shape from the **AutoShapes** tool. Click and drag below your lever to draw a circle that represents a wheel. (Figure 7-10).

Lever

Figure 7-10

16. Next, click on your circle, select the **3-D tool**, and choose **3-D Style 1** (Figure 7-11). Your circle should now resemble a wheel.

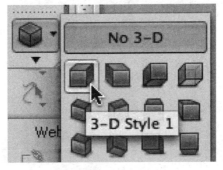

Figure 7-11

Simple Machines Diagram (cont.)
Activity 7

17. Now select the **Cylinder** shape from the **Shapes** tool. Use it to draw a short, thin cylinder below your circle (Figure 7-12).

Figure 7-12

18. Click on the cylinder, then choose the **Free Rotate** tool, and use it to rotate the cylinder so it appears like an axle. Click the **Free Rotate** tool to turn it off, then click and drag the cylinder over your wheel so your drawing resembles a wheel and axle. (Figure 7-13).

Figure 7-13

19. Use the **Text Box** tool to label your wheel and axle.

20. Now you will draw a gear. From the **AutoShapes** tool, select **Stars and Banners** and choose the **32 Point Star** shape. Click and drag below your inclined plane to draw a star that represents a gear. Make your gear three-dimensional by using the **3-D** button (Figure 7-14).

Figure 7-14

21. Use the **Text Box** tool to label your gear.

Simple Machines Diagram (cont.)
Activity 7

22. Now you will draw a pulley. From the **AutoShapes** tool, select the **Circle** shape. Use it to draw two small circles, one on top of the other, below your wheel and axle (Figure 7-15).

Figure 7-15

23. Next, use the **Circle** shape tool to draw two smaller circles inside of the two circles you just drew. Then, use the **Line** tool to draw two lines that represent rope connecting the two pulleys (Figure 7-16).

Figure 7-16

24. Use the **Text Box** tool to label your pulley.

25. Now you will draw a screw. From the **AutoShapes** tool, select the **Trapezoid** shape (Figure 7-17).

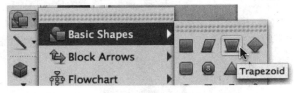

Figure 7-17

26. Click and drag the trapezoid straight down just below your gear to draw a long narrow trapezoid (Figure 7-18).

Figure 7-18

Simple Machines Diagram *(cont.)*
Activity 7

27. Double-click on your trapezoid, and choose **Colors and Lines**. Select **Fill Color**, and choose **Fill Effects**. Choose **Pattern** and **Wide upward diagonal** (Figure 7-19).

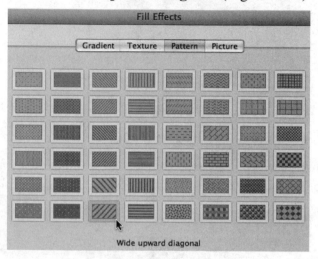

Figure 7-19

28. Next, use the **Circle** shapes tool to draw an oval on the top of your screw. Then choose a **Four Point Star** from the **Stars** shapes tool and draw a small star in the middle of your oval to make a screw head (Figure 7-20).

Figure 7-20

29. Use the **Text Box** tool to label your screw.

30. Next, you will use the **Triangle** shapes tool to draw a wedge at the center of your page below your screw and pulley. Use the **Free Rotate** to rotate your triangle 180 degrees. Lastly, use the **Text Box** tool to label your wedge.

31. Your project is now complete!

Unit Conversion
Activity 8

Objectives

Each student will utilize a spreadsheet program to create a unit conversion calculator to convert English units to metric units, and metric units to English units.

Benchmarks for Technology Standards

Students will know the characteristics, uses, and basic features of computer software programs, including:

- knowing the common features and uses of spreadsheets
- using spreadsheet software to update, add, and delete data, and to produce charts

Learning Objectives

At the end of this lesson, students will be able to:

1. Create a new spreadsheet document.
2. Know the various terms associated with spreadsheets, including *rows*, *columns*, and *cells*.
3. Enter data into a spreadsheet.
4. Adjust the alignment of data within a cell.
5. Enter formulas into a cell.
6. Use cell formulas to calculate English/metric unit conversions.
7. Enter a header into a spreadsheet.

Before the Computer

This activity can be completed using most versions of Microsoft Excel, Open Office, and iWorks. Make sure to try the activity with your school's spreadsheet software and be prepared to modify the procedures accordingly.

Variations

Depending on the age and ability level of your students, you may wish to have students enter the conversions from Metric to English as shown in Table 8-2, or you can also add other unit conversion formulas as well. An example of a completed spreadsheet is shown in Figure 8-1.

Value	Unit	Equals	Value	Unit
2	Miles	=	3.2	Kilometers
3	Feet	=	0.9	Meters
1	Inches	=	2.5	Centimeters
1	Liquid Ounces	=	29.6	Milliliters
1	Gallons	=	3.79	Liters
1	Dry Ounces	=	28.35	Grams
1	Pounds	=	0.453	Kilograms

Figure 8-1

Unit Conversion (cont.)
Activity 8

Procedure

1. Open a new spreadsheet document. Spreadsheets are made up of columns that are identified by letters (A, B, C, etc.) and rows that are identified by numbers (1, 2, 3, etc.).

2. The location within a spreadsheet where a column meets a row is called a cell, and is identified by both a letter and number (Figure 8-2).

Figure 8-2

3. Click into cell **A1**, and type in the following label: "Value."

4. Hit the **tab** key on your keyboard to bring you to cell B1, and type "Unit."

5. Continue to fill in the remaining labels in row 1 as shown in Figure 8-3.

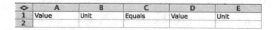

	A	B	C	D	E
1	Value	Unit	Equals	Value	Unit
2					

Figure 8-3

6. Click and drag over all of the labels in row 1 to highlight them, then use the **Bold** and **Align Center** buttons on your tool bar to make the labels bold and centered in each cell (Figure 8-4).

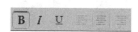

Figure 8-4

7. Next, click into cell **B2** and type "Miles." Hit the **tab** key on your keyboard to move you into cell **C2** and type in "=," then skip over into cell **E2** and type "Kilometers."

8. Now you are going to enter a formula into cell D2 that will calculate the conversion of miles into kilometers. Click into cell **D2** and enter the following formula: **=A2*1.6**. This formula will multiply the number entered into cell A2 by 1.6 and display the answer in cell D2. Hit the **enter** key on your keyboard and then click into cell **A2** and type in 1. The conversion to kilometers should automatically calculate in cell D2 (1.6).

9. Try typing the number 2 into cell **A2** and hit **enter**. The answer in kilometers should now show as 3.2.

10. Next, click into cell **B3** and type "Feet." hit the tab key on your keyboard to move into cell **C3** and type "=," then skip over into cell **E3** and type "Meters."

11. Now click into cell **D3** and enter the following formula for converting feet into meters: **=A3*0.3**. Hit the **enter** key on your keyboard, click into cell **A3**, and type "3." Cell D3 should now show the conversion as 0.9 Meters.

Unit Conversion *(cont.)*
Activity 8

12. Next, fill in the remaining conversions into your spreadsheet using the formulas shown in Table 8-1.

English/Metric Conversion Formulas
miles * 1.6 = kilometers
feet * 0.3 = meters
inches * 2.5 = centimeters
liquid ounces * 29.6 = milliliters
gallons * 3.79 = liters
dry ounces * 28.35 = grams
pounds * 0.453 = kilograms

Table 8-1

13. Once you have entered all of your formulas, highlight all of the cells in your spreadsheet and center all of the data and labels in the cells using the **Align Center** button on your toolbar.

14. Finally, you will insert a header into your spreadsheet. To do this, go to the **View** menu, and select **Header/Footer.** Click on **Customize Header**, and enter the following into the Center Section window: "English/Metric Conversion."

15. If you have time, enter the conversions for Metric/English as shown in Table 8-2 into your spreadsheet.

Metric/English Conversion Formulas
kilometers / 1.6 = miles
meters / 0.3 = miles
centimeters / 2.5 = inches
milliliters / 29.6 = ounces
liters / 3.79 = gallons
grams / 28.35 = ounces
kilograms / 0.453 = pounds

Table 8-2

16. Your project is now complete!

Area Formulas
Activity 9

Objectives

Each student will utilize a spreadsheet program to create an area formula calculator to determine the area of five different geometric shapes, including a square, rectangle, circle, parallelogram, and triangle.

Benchmarks for Technology Standards

Students will know the characteristics, uses, and basic features of computer software programs, including:

- knowing the common features and uses of spreadsheets
- using spreadsheet software to update, add, and delete data and to produce charts

Learning Objectives

At the end of this lesson, students will be able to:

1. Create a new spreadsheet document.
2. Know the various terms associated with spreadsheets, including *rows*, *columns*, and *cells*.
3. Adjust the width of columns within a spreadsheet.
4. Enter data into a spreadsheet.
5. Adjust the alignment of data within a cell.
6. Enter formulas into a cell.
7. Use cell formulas to calculate the area of a square, rectangle, parallelogram, circle, and triangle.
8. Enter a header into a spreadsheet.

Before the Computer

This activity can be completed using most versions of Microsoft Excel, Open Office, and iWorks. Make sure to try the activity with your school's spreadsheet software, and be prepared to modify the procedures accordingly.

Variations

Depending on the age and ability level of your students, you may wish to have students enter other mathematical formulas that they are studying into their spreadsheets. An example of a completed spreadsheet is shown in Figure 9-1.

Area Calculations

Length of Square=	5	Area of Square =	25		
Length of Rectangle =	5	Width of Rectangle =	10	Area of Rectangle =	50
Radius of Circle =	10	Area of Circle =	314		
Base of Parallelogram =	5	Height of Parallelogram	10	Area of Parallelogram=	50
Base of Triangle =	15	Height of Triangle =	20	Area of Triangle =	150

Figure 9-1

Area Formulas (cont.)
Activity 9

Procedure

1. Open a new spreadsheet document. Spreadsheets are made up of columns that are identified by letters (A, B, C, etc.) and rows that are identified by numbers (1, 2, 3, etc.).

2. The location within a spreadsheet where a column meets a row is called a cell and is identified by both a letter and number (Figure 9-2).

Figure 9-2

3. Click into cell **A1**, and type in the following label: "Length of Square =." You will now have to adjust the width of your column to make it large enough to read the text you just entered. To do this, move your cursor to the line separating columns A and B, then click and drag your mouse to widen the column (Figure 9-3).

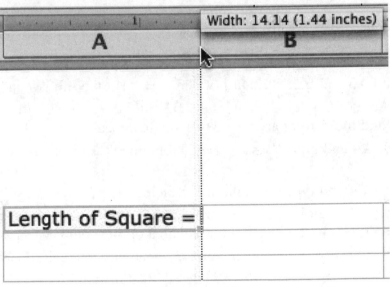

Figure 9-3

4. After you have widened your column enough to read the text within the cell, hit the **tab** key on your keyboard to bring you to cell **B1**, and type in the number 5. This time reduce the width of the column.

5. Hit the **tab** key once again to bring you to cell **C1**, and type "Area of Square =." You may have to adjust your column width using the same procedure you used for column A.

Area Formulas (cont.)
Activity 9

6. Move into cell **D1** and enter in the following formula: **=B1*B1**. This formula will multiply the value typed into cell B1 by itself, which will determine its area. Hit the **enter** key on your keyboard, and the correct area of **25** should appear in cell D1 (Figure 9-4). You should also reduce the width of the column.

Length of Square =	5	Area of Square =	25

Figure 9-4

7. Click and drag over all of the cells in row 1 to highlight them, and then use the **Align Center** button on your toolbar to center the text in each cell.

8. Next, click into cell **A2** and type "Length of Rectangle =." Hit the **tab** key on your keyboard to move into cell **B2** and type "5," then hit the **tab** key to bring you to cell **C2** and type "Width of Rectangle =."

9. Click into cell **D2** and enter "10," then click into **E2** and type "Area of Rectangle =."

10. Adjust the column widths so all text is visible.

11. Now you are going to enter a formula into cell **F2** that will calculate the area of a rectangle. The formula is **=B2*D2**. Hit the **enter** key on your keyboard.

12. Center all of the data in row 2 (Figure 9-5).

Length of Square =	5	Area of Square =	25		
Length of Rectangle =	5	Width of Rectangle =	10	Area of Rectangle =	50

Figure 9-5

13. Next, click into cell **A3** and type, "Radius of Circle =." Hit the **tab** key and in cell **B3** type "10."

14. In cell **C3**, type "Area of Circle =," then in cell **D3** enter the following formula: **=(B3*B3)*3.14**. Hit the **enter** key and the correct area of "314" should appear.

15. Now click into cell **A4** and type "Base of Parallelogram =." Hit the **tab** key and enter "5" into cell **B4**.

16. Now move into cell **C4** and type, "Height of Parallelogram =," then in cell **D4** enter "10."

17. Next, in cell **E4**, type "Area of Parallelogram =," then enter the following formula in cell **F4: = B4*D4** and hit the **enter** key. The correct area of **50** should appear.

18. Click into cell **A5** and enter "Base of Triangle =," then click into cell **B5** and type "15."

19. Move into cell **C5** and type "Height of Triangle =," then in cell **D5** type "20."

20. Finally, in cell **E5** type "Area of Triangle =," and then in cell **F5** enter the following formula: **= (B5*D5)*0.5**. The correct area of **150** should appear.

21. Now you will insert a header into your spreadsheet. To do this, go to the **View** menu and select **Header/Footer**. Click on **Customize Header** and enter the following into the Center Section window: "Area Calculations."

22. Your project is now complete!

Mean, Median, Range, and Mode
Activity 10

Objectives

Each student will enter number data into a spreadsheet and then use functions to calculate the data's Mean, Median, Range, and Mode.

Benchmarks for Technology Standards

Students will know the characteristics, uses, and basic features of computer software programs, including:

- knowing the common features and uses of spreadsheets
- using spreadsheet software to update, add, and delete data and to produce charts

Learning Objectives

At the end of this lesson, students will be able to:

1. Create a new spreadsheet document.
2. Know the various terms associated with spreadsheets, including *rows, columns,* and *cells*.
3. Adjust the width of columns within a spreadsheet.
4. Enter data into a spreadsheet.
5. Adjust the alignment of data within a cell.
6. Change the format of the font within a spreadsheet.
7. Enter a formula into a spreadsheet.
8. Use the average, median, and mode functions in a spreadsheet.

Before the Computer

This activity can be completed using most versions of Microsoft Excel, Open Office, and iWorks. The procedure for selecting functions in a spreadsheet may vary depending on the software and version your school uses. Make sure to try the activity with your school's spreadsheet software, and be prepared to modify the procedure accordingly.

Variations

Depending on the age and ability level of your students, you may wish to have students collect their own data to use in order to determine the mean, median, range, and mode. An example of a completed spreadsheet is shown in Figure 10-1.

Mean, Median, Range, and Mode (cont.)
Activity 10

◇	A	B
1	**Student**	**Price of Backpack**
2	Zack	$35.00
3	Grace	$21.00
4	Helen	$19.00
5	Miranda	$38.00
6	Jonas	$24.00
7	Charlotte	$20.00
8	Kyle	$39.00
9	Brendan	$17.00
10	Nate	$15.00
11	Lauren	$38.00
12	Forest	$20.00
13	Zoe	$16.00
14	Elizabeth	$42.00
15	Nell	$26.00
16		
17	**Mean**	$26.43
18	**Median**	$22.50
19	**Range**	$27.00
20	**Mode**	$38.00
21		

Figure 10-1

Mean, Median, Range, and Mode *(cont.)*
Activity 10

Procedure

1. Open a new spreadsheet document. Spreadsheets are made up of columns that are identified by letters (A, B, C, etc.) and rows that are identified by numbers (1, 2, 3, etc.).

2. The location within a spreadsheet where a column meets a row is called a cell and is identified by both a letter and number (Figure 10-2).

Figure 10-2

3. Click into cell **A1**, and type in the following label: "Student." Hit the **tab** key on your keyboard to bring you over, to cell **B2**, and type in the label: "Price of Backpack." Continue to fill in each remaining student's name in Column A.

4. Next, click and drag over the two column labels and use the **Bold** button on your toolbar.

5. Now fill in the data in the appropriate columns for each student and the cost of his or her backpack, as shown in Figure 10-3.

	A	B
1	**Student**	**Price of Backpack**
2	Zack	35
3	Grace	21
4	Helen	19
5	Miranda	38
6	Jonas	24
7	Charlotte	20
8	Kyle	39
9	Brendan	17
10	Nate	15
11	Lauren	38
12	Forest	20
13	Zoe	16
14	Elizabeth	42
15	Nell	26

Figure 10-3

Mean, Median, Range, and Mode (cont.)
Activity 10

6. Now you will center the data in your cells. To do this, you click and drag over all of your data to highlight it. Then use the **Align Center** button on your toolbar.

7. You may also have to widen column B so that you can read its label. To do this, take your cursor and move it to the line separating columns B and C, then click and drag your mouse to widen the column (Figure 10-4).

	A	B	C
			Width: 14.29 (1.46 inches)
	Student	**Price of Backpack**	
	Zack	35	
	Grace	21	

Figure 10-4

8. Next, you are going to change the format of the numbers in the Price of Backpack column so they appear with a dollar value. Click and drag over all of the numbers in column B to highlight them. Choose the **Format** menu, select **Cells**, click on the **Number** tab or button, and select **Currency**. Click **OK**, and all of your numbers should now be displayed with dollar signs.

9. Now you are going to insert a function, which will calculate the mean cost of all the backpacks. Click into cell **A17** and type "Mean." Make this label bold.

10. Hit the **tab** key on your keyboard to move into cell B17. Go to the **Insert** menu, and select **Function**. Locate the **AVERAGE** function and double-click on it. The average or mean formula should appear like this in cell B17: **=AVERAGE(B2:B16)**.

11. Change the **B16** to **B15** and hit the **enter** key on your keyboard. This instructs the function to calculate the average of the numbers in cells B2 through B15. The mean for your data should now be displayed in cell B17 as $26.43 (Figure 10-5).

14	Elizabeth	$42.00
15	Nell	$26.00
16		
17	**Mean**	$26.43

Figure 10-5

12. Next, click in cell **A18** and type "Median." Make this label bold, and hit the **tab** key to move over to cell **B18**. This time select the **Median** function, and then click and drag over the cell numbers in between the parentheses to highlight them (Figure 10-6).

17	**Mean**	$26.43
18	**Median**	=MEDIAN(B17)
19		MEDIAN(number1, [number2], ...)
20		

Figure 10-6

Mean, Median, Range, and Mode (cont.)
Activity 10

13. With the numbers still highlighted, click and drag over the price of the backpacks from cell **B2** through **B15**, then hit the **enter** key. This should automatically change the numbers within the Median function to B2:B15. Hit the **enter** key again, and the median number for your backpack cost should display as $22.50.

14. Now you are going to enter in a function to calculate the range of your backpack cost. Click into cell **A19** and type, "Range." Make it bold, and then hit the tab key. The range is the difference between the highest and lowest values. The highest cost of the backpacks is $42, which is in cell B14. The lowest cost is $15, which is in Cell **B10**. In cell **B19**, enter the following formula to calculate the range: **=B14-B10**. Hit the **enter** key, and the range of $27 should be displayed.

15. Finally, you are going to determine the mode for your backpack costs. Click into cell **A20** and type "Mode." Make it bold, and then hit the **tab** key to move into cell **B20**.

16. Insert the mode function, and then highlight the numbers in between the parentheses. With the numbers still highlighted, click and drag over the price of the backpacks from cell **B2** through **B15**, then hit the **enter** key. This should automatically change the numbers within the Mode function to **B2:B15**. Hit the **enter** key again, and the mode number for your backpack cost should display as $38.00.

17. Your project is now complete!

Climograph Line-Column Chart
Activity 11

Objectives

Each student will use climate data gathered from the Internet to create a climograph line-column chart showing the monthly average temperature and precipitation over the period of a year for a city near his or her school.

Benchmarks for Technology Standards

Students will know the characteristics, uses, and basic features of computer software programs, including:

- knowing the common features and uses of spreadsheets
- using spreadsheet software to update, add, and delete data, and to produce charts

Learning Objectives

At the end of this lesson, students will be able to:

1. Create a new spreadsheet document.
2. Know the various terms associated with spreadsheets, including *rows*, *columns*, and *cells*.
3. Use the Internet to gather climate information.
4. Utilize the Autofill function to automatically enter the months of the year into a column of a spreadsheet.
5. Adjust the width of columns within a spreadsheet.
6. Enter data into a spreadsheet.
7. Adjust the alignment and style of the font within a spreadsheet.
8. Create and format a line-column chart from data entered within a spreadsheet.

Before the Computer

- This activity can be completed using most versions of Microsoft Excel, Open Office, and iWorks. The procedure for formatting charts using spreadsheets may vary depending on the software and version your school uses. Make sure to try the activity with your school's spreadsheet software, and be prepared to modify the chart procedure accordingly.
- Make sure the following website is accessible to your class prior to teaching the lesson: http://www.worldclimate.com.

Variations

Depending on the age and ability level of your students, you may wish to have students create more than one climograph. Choosing two cities that are in different parts of the country could be a good way to show how climate affects the local ecosystem. An example of a completed column chart is shown in Figure 11-1.

Climograph Line-Column Chart *(cont.)*
Activity 11

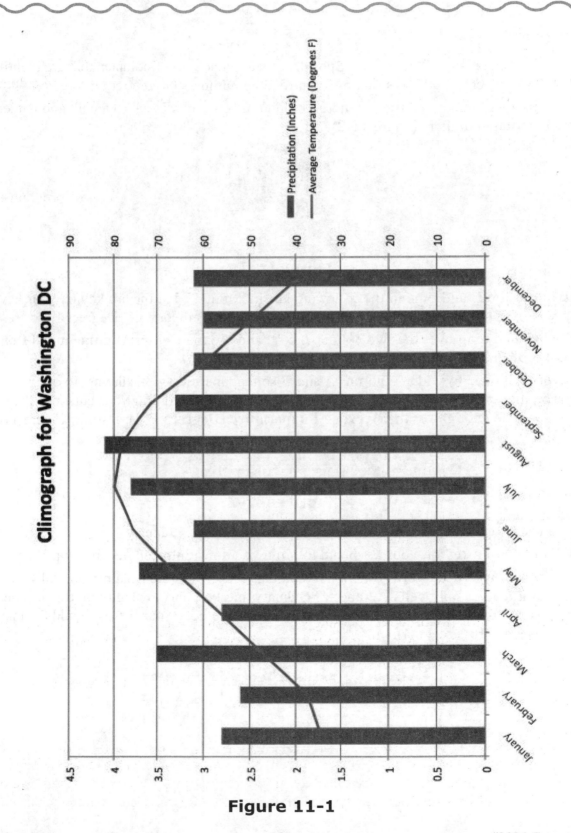

Figure 11-1

Climograph Line-Column Chart (cont.)
Activity 11

Procedure

1. Open a new spreadsheet document. Spreadsheets are made up of columns that are identified by letters (A, B, C, etc.) and rows that are identified by numbers (1, 2, 3, etc.).

2. The location within a spreadsheet where a column meets a row is called a cell, and is identified by both a letter and number (Figure 11-2).

Figure 11-2

3. Click into cell **A1**, and type in the following label: "Month." Hit the **tab** key on your keyboard to bring you over to cell **B1**, and type in the label "Average Temperature (Degrees F)."

4. Next, click and drag over the two column labels, and use the **Center Alignment** and **Bold** buttons on your toolbar.

5. Now you will have to widen columns A and B so the label fits within them. To do this, place your cursor on the line separating columns B and C. Then, click and drag your cursor to the right until the cell is wide enough for the **Average Temperature** (**Degrees F**) label to fit (Figure 11-3).

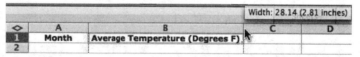

Figure 11-3

6. Next, click into cell **A2** and enter the first month of the year, "January."

7. Now hit the **enter** key on your keyboard to bring you down into cell **A3**, then type "February."

8. Next, you will use the Autofill function to automatically fill in the remaining months. To do this, click and drag over only cells **A2** and **A3** (January and February) to highlight them. Then, move your cursor to the bottom right corner over the little blue dot. Your cursor should then appear as a small plus sign (Figure 11-4).

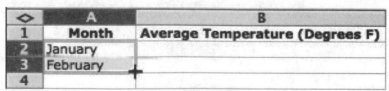

Figure 11-4

58

Climograph Line-Column Chart (cont.)
Activity 11

9. Once the plus sign appears at the corner of cell **A3**, click and drag down column A until your cursor arrives at cell **A13**. The remaining months of the year should have automatically filled into column A (Figure 11-5).

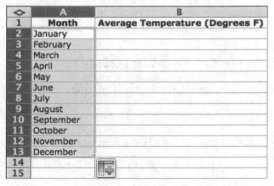

Figure 11-5

10. Next, you will need to use the Internet to retrieve data on average temperatures. Open up your web browser and navigate to the following website: **www.worldclimate.com**.

11. Once you arrive at the website, type in the city you are going to use for your climograph, and hit the **search** button. In this example, we will use Washington DC.

12. Your search should reveal many different place names with climate data for the name of your desired city. Click on one of the links that best represents your location. Now go through the list of climate data, and select **24 hr. Average Temperature**.

13. A table showing the average temperature for each month of the year should now appear in a new window. Use the data in Fahrenheit, and enter the temperature value for each month as shown on the website into your spreadsheet.

14. Once your data has been entered, click into cell **C1** and type in the following label, "Precipitation (inches)." Center and make bold, and also adjust the column width so it is wide enough to read.

15. Return to the website and go back one page, and select the **Average Rainfall** link.

16. A table showing the average rainfall for each month of the year should now appear in a new window. Use the data in inches, and enter the precipitation value for each month as shown on the website into your spreadsheet.

17. Now that you have all of the data on temperature and precipitation in your spreadsheet, you will create a climograph in the form of a line-column graph.

18. Click and drag over all of the data in your spreadsheet to highlight it. Go to the **Insert** menu and select **Chart**. Choose a **Line-Column** chart. (If you are using Excel 2007 or 2008, you will need to create a column chart, then select the "Precipitation (inches)" series in the chart itself and click on the **line chart** option.) Your chart title should be the name of the city you used for your climograph, for example: "Climograph of Washington DC."

19. Your project is now complete!

Star Temperature Scatter Chart
Activity 12

Objectives

Each student will use data on the temperature of stars entered into a spreadsheet to create a scatter chart.

Benchmarks for Technology Standards

Students will know the characteristics, uses, and basic features of computer software programs, including:

- knowing the common features and uses of spreadsheets
- using spreadsheet software to update, add, and delete data and to produce charts

Learning Objectives

At the end of this lesson, students will be able to:

1. Create a new spreadsheet document.
2. Know the various terms associated with spreadsheets, including *rows*, *columns*, and *cells*.
3. Adjust the width of columns within a spreadsheet.
4. Enter data into a spreadsheet.
5. Adjust the alignment and style of the font within a spreadsheet.
6. Create a scatter chart from data entered within a spreadsheet.
7. Change the background and data point format of a scatter chart.

Before the Computer

This activity can be completed using most versions of Microsoft Excel, Open Office, and iWorks. The procedure for formatting charts using spreadsheets may vary depending on the software and version your school uses. Make sure to try the activity with your school's spreadsheet software, and be prepared to modify the chart procedure accordingly.

Variations

Depending on the age and ability level of your students, you may wish to have students to enter more data on additional stars. An example of a completed scatter chart is shown in Figure 12-1.

Star Temperature Scatter Chart *(cont.)*
Activity 12

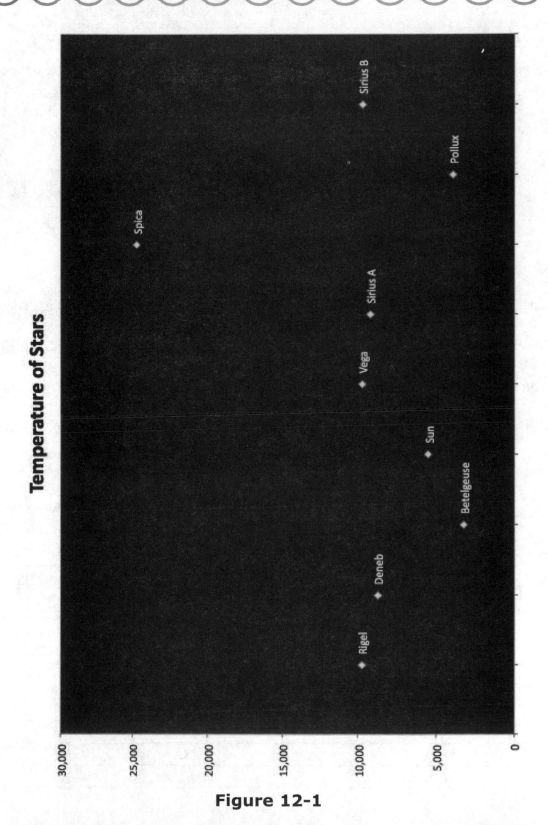

Figure 12-1

Star Temperature Scatter Chart *(cont.)*
Activity 12

Procedure

1. Open a new spreadsheet document. Spreadsheets are made up of columns that are identified by letters (A, B, C, etc.) and rows that are identified by numbers (1, 2, 3, etc.).

2. The location within a spreadsheet where a column meets a row is called a cell and is identified by both a letter and number (Figure 12-2).

Figure 12-2

3. Click into cell **A1**, and type the label "Star." Hit the **tab** key on your keyboard to bring you over to cell **B1**, and type in the label "Temperature (Degrees C)."

4. Next, click and drag over the two column labels, and use the **Center Alignment** and **Bold** buttons on your toolbar.

5. Now you will have to widen column B so you are able to read the label. To do this, place your cursor on the line separating columns B and C. Then click and drag your cursor to the right until the cell is wide enough for the "Temperature (Degrees C)" label to fit in (Figure 12-3).

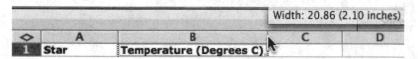

Figure 12-3

6. Next, enter the data on star temperatures from the table below into your spreadsheet.

Star	Temperature (Degrees C)
Rigel	9,727
Deneb	8,727
Betelgeuse	3,727
Sun	5,727
Vega	9,727
Sirius A	9,727
Spica	24,727
Pollux	3,727
Sirius B	9,727

Star Temperature Scatter Chart *(cont.)*
Activity 12

7. Highlight your data by clicking and dragging over it, and then select the **Insert** menu and choose **Chart**. Select the **X-Y Scatter chart, Points Only**. (For Excel 2007 or 2008, select **Marked Scatter**.)

8. Click **Next**, and change the chart title so it reads, **Temperature of Stars.**

9. Under **Axes**, remove the X-axis. (For Excel 2007 or 2008, this is in the Formatting Palette.)

10. Under **Gridlines**, remove both major and minor gridlines.

11. Under **Legend**, remove the checkmark from **Legend** or choose **None**.

12. Under **Data Labels** choose **Category Name** or **X-Values**.

13. Finally, click **Next** and save your chart as a **New Sheet.** You can also go to the **Chart** menu and select **Move Chart** to save as a new sheet (Figure 12-4).

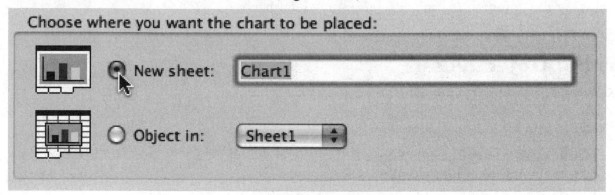

Figure 12-4

14. Your scatter chart should now be displayed. Next, you are going to change the color of your data points. To do this, double-click on one of the data points in your chart. Change the **Marker Fill** (both background and foreground) to a bright yellow. Click **OK**.

15. Now you will change the color of your chart's data labels. To do this, double-click on one of the data labels in your chart and change its font color to bright yellow. Click **OK**.

16. Finally, you will change the background color of your chart. To do this, double-click on your chart's background to bring up the **Format Plot Area** window, and change the **Plot Area** or **Fill** to black. Click **OK**.

17. Your project is now complete!

Beach Garbage Doughnut Chart
Activity 13

Objectives

Each student will use data collected on the type and amount of garbage collected in 2008 on beaches around the world during the 24th Annual International Coastal Cleanup to create an exploded doughnut chart using a spreadsheet application.

Benchmarks for Technology Standards

Students will know the characteristics, uses, and basic features of computer software programs, including:

- knowing the common features and uses of spreadsheets
- using spreadsheet software to update, add, and delete data and to produce charts

Learning Objectives

At the end of this lesson, students will be able to:

1. Create a new spreadsheet document.
2. Know the various terms associated with spreadsheets, including *rows*, *columns*, and *cells*.
3. Adjust the width of columns within a spreadsheet.
4. Enter data into a spreadsheet.
5. Adjust the alignment of data within a cell.
6. Change the style of the font within a spreadsheet.
7. Create and format an exploded doughnut chart from data entered within a spreadsheet.
8. Move a label within a chart.

Before the Computer

This activity can be completed using most versions of Microsoft Excel, Open Office, and iWorks. The procedure for formatting charts using spreadsheets may vary depending on the software and version your school uses. Make sure to try the activity with your school's spreadsheet software, and be prepared to modify the chart procedure accordingly.

Variations

Depending on the age and ability level of your students, you may wish to have students visit **oceanconservancy.org** and have them get additional data on the type and amount of garbage collected from beaches around the world. An example of a completed doughnut chart is shown in Figure 13-1.

Beach Garbage Doughnut Chart (cont.)
Activity 13

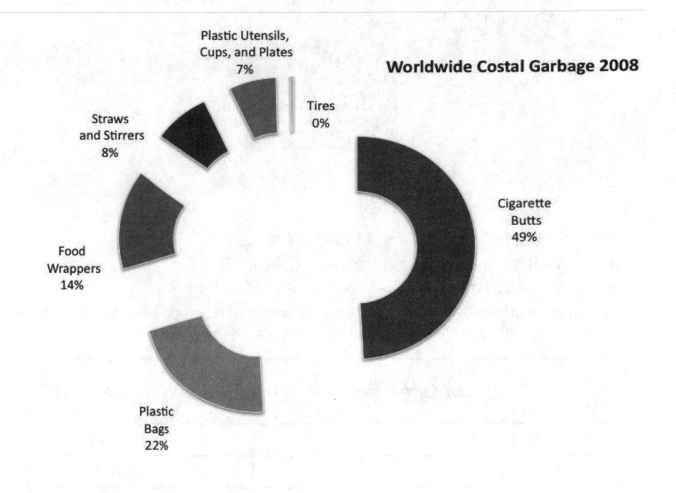

Figure 13-1

Beach Garbage Doughnut Chart (cont.)
Activity 13

Procedure

1. Begin this activity by opening a new spreadsheet document. Spreadsheets are made up of columns that are identified by letters (A, B, C, etc.) and rows that are identified by numbers (1, 2, 3, etc.).

2. The location within a spreadsheet where a column meets a row is called a cell and is identified by both a letter and number (Figure 13-2).

Figure 13-2

3. Click into cell **A1**, and type the label "Type of Garbage."

4. Next click into cell **B1** and type the label "Amount of Garbage."

5. Now fill in the name of the type of garbage collected from the world's beaches in column A and the amount of garbage collected in column B using the following data.

Type of Garbage	Amount of Garbage
Cigarette Butts	3,200,000
Plastic Bags	1,400,000
Food Wrappers	942,620
Straws and Stirrers	509,593
Plastic Utensils, Cups, and Plates	441,053
Tires	26,585

6. Next, click and drag over the two column labels, and use the **Bold** button on your toolbar.

Beach Garbage Doughnut Chart *(cont.)*
Activity 13

7. Now you will center the data in your cells. To do this, click and drag over all of your data to highlight it. Then use the **Align Center** button on your toolbar.

8. Next, you will have to widen columns A and B so the label fits within them. To do this, place your cursor on the line separating columns A and B. Then click and drag your cursor to the right until the cell is wide enough for the "Type of Garbage" label to fit within it (Figure 13-3).

Figure 13-3

9. Repeat the same process to widen column B so you can read the "Amount of Garbage" label.

10. Now you are going to use your data to create a chart. First, highlight all of your data in both columns, including the labels. Choose the **Insert** menu and select **Chart**, then **Exploded Doughnut** (Figure 13-4).

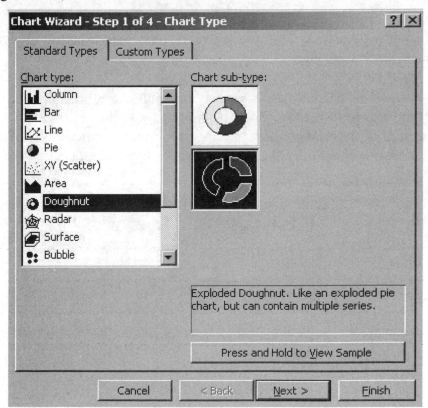

Figure 13-4

Beach Garbage Doughnut Chart (cont.)
Activity 13

11. Click **Next**, and an example of your chart should appear. Click the **Next** button again to display the **Chart Options** window.

12. Click on the **Titles** tab and type "Worldwide Coastal Garbage 2008."

13. Click on the **Legend tab,** and remove the checkmark from the **Show Legend** box.

14. Click on the **Data Labels** tab and put checkmarks in the boxes labeled **Category Name and Percent**. Then click the small arrow next to **Separator** and choose **New Line**.

15. Click the **Next** button, check next to **New sheet**, and click **Finish**. You can also go to the **Chart** menu and select **Move Chart** to save as a new sheet (Figure 13-5).

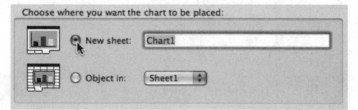

Figure 13-5

16. Your chart should now be displayed. Sometimes it is necessary to make the font size of the labels on a chart larger so they are easier to read. To do this, double-click on one of the labels to bring up the **Format Data Labels** window. Now change the font size to **12**, and then click **OK**.

17. Once you change the font size of the labels in a doughnut chart, you might have to move them so they are not too crowded together and unreadable. To do this, click once on one of the chart's labels to highlight all of them, then click once again on the specific label you want to move. A text box should appear around only that specific label. Now you can click and drag it to a new location (Figure 13-6).

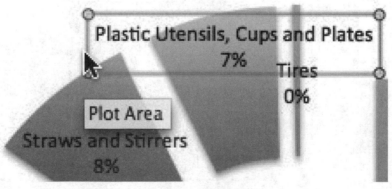

Figure 13-6

18. Once you have moved your label so it is readable, click anywhere on your chart to leave the label's edit mode.

19. Your project is now complete!

Carbon Dioxide Line Chart
Activity 14

Objectives

Each student will use data gathered on the levels of carbon dioxide within the atmosphere to create a three-dimensional line chart. He or she will also learn how to use the Autofill function within a spreadsheet to automatically insert a series of dates.

Benchmarks for Technology Standards

Students will know the characteristics, uses, and basic features of computer software programs, including:

- knowing the common features and uses of spreadsheets
- using spreadsheet software to update, add, and delete data, and to produce charts

Learning Objectives

At the end of this lesson, students will be able to:

1. Create a new spreadsheet document.
2. Know the various terms associated with spreadsheets, including *rows*, *columns*, and *cells*.
3. Use the Internet to gather climate information.
4. Utilize the Autofill function to automatically enter a series of years into a column of a spreadsheet.
5. Adjust the width of columns within a spreadsheet.
6. Enter data into a spreadsheet.
7. Adjust the alignment and style of the font within a spreadsheet.
8. Create and format a 3D line chart from data entered within a spreadsheet.
9. Change the x-axis labels of a chart.

Before the Computer

This activity can be completed using most versions of Microsoft Excel, Open Office, and iWorks. The procedure for formatting charts using spreadsheets may vary depending on the software and version your school uses. Make sure to try the activity with your school's spreadsheet software, and be prepared to modify the chart procedure accordingly.

Variations

Depending on the age and ability level of your students, you may wish to have students enter data into their spreadsheet going further back in time. The Carbon Dioxide Information Analysis Center website has data on atmospheric carbon dioxide levels going all the way back to 1958. Use the following webpage to access this data to create a more detailed line graph:

http://cdiac.ornl.gov/

An example of a completed line chart is shown in Figure 14-1.

Carbon Dioxide Line Chart (cont.)
Activity 14

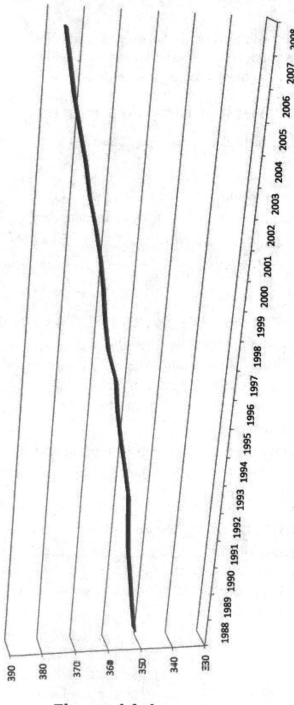

Figure 14-1

Carbon Dioxide Line Chart *(cont.)*
Activity 14

Procedure

1. Open a new spreadsheet document. Spreadsheets are made up of columns that are identified by letters (A, B, C, etc.) and rows that are identified by numbers (1, 2, 3, etc.).

2. The location within a spreadsheet where a column meets a row is called a cell and is identified by both a letter and number (Figure 14-2).

Figure 14-2

3. Click into cell **A1**, and type in the following label, "Year." Hit the **tab** key on your keyboard to bring you over to cell **B1**, and type in the label **"Average Annual Atmospheric Carbon Dioxide (ppm)."**

4. Next, click and drag over the two column labels, and use the **Center Alignment** and **Bold** buttons on your toolbar.

5. Now you will have to widen column B so the label fits within it. To do this, place your cursor on the line separating columns B and C. Then click and drag your cursor to the right until the cell is wide enough for the "Average Annual Atmospheric Carbon Dioxide (ppm)" label to fit in (Figure 14-3).

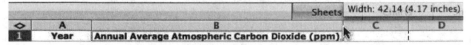

Figure 14-3

6. Next, click into cell **A2** and enter the first year you are going to use, "1988."

7. Now hit the **enter** key on your keyboard to bring you down into cell **A3**, and type "1989."

8. Next, you will use the **Autofill** function to automatically fill in the remaining years. To do this, click and drag over only cells **A2** and **A3** (1988 and 1989) to highlight them. Then move your cursor to the bottom right corner over the little blue dot. Your cursor should then appear as a small plus sign (Figure 14-4).

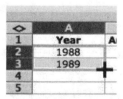

Figure 14-4

Carbon Dioxide Line Chart (cont.)
Activity 14

9. Once the plus sign appears at the corner of cell **A3**, click and drag down column **A** until your cursor arrives at cell **A22**. The remaining years should have automatically filled into column A (Figure 14-5).

Figure 14-5

10. Next, use the data table below to type in the level of carbon dioxide in the atmosphere for the period between 1988 and 2008.

Year	Annual Average Atmospheric Carbon Dioxed (ppm)
1988	351.48
1989	352.91
1990	354.19
1991	355.59
1992	356.37
1993	357.04
1994	358.89
1995	360.88
1996	362.64
1997	363.76
1998	366.63
1999	368.31
2000	369.48
2001	371.02
2002	373.10
2003	375.64
2004	377.38
2005	379.67
2006	381.84
2007	383.55
2008	385.34

Carbon Dioxide Line Chart *(cont.)*
Activity 14

11. Once you have entered in all of your data on carbon dioxide, click and drag over all of your labels and data, then select the **Insert** menu and choose **Chart**.

12. Choose the **3-D Line** chart, and click **Next**. Now you will have to remove the year data from your chart. In the **Select Data Source** window, click on **Year** in the **Series** window and hit **Remove** (Figure 14-6). You can also get to this window by choosing the **Chart** menu and selecting **Source Data**.

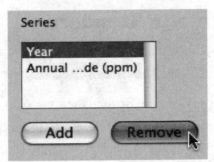

Figure 14-6

13. Now, you will set up your x-axis labels in the same Select Data Source window. Click on the small red arrow icon next to the **Category (X) Axis Labels** window (Figure 14-7).

Figure 14-7

14. After you click on the red arrow icon, click and drag over only the years in column A of your spreadsheet, hit the **enter** key on your keyboard, and then hit **Next**, or hit **OK**.

15. Now you are going to label your chart. Change the title of your chart to "Atmospheric Carbon Dioxide." Your x-axis label should be "Year," and the y-axis label "ppm."

16. Click on the **Legend** tab and remove the checkmark from **Show Legend**, or choose **None**.

17. Click **Next** and now you are going choose to save your chart as a **New Sheet** and click **OK**.(Figure 14-8). You can also select the **Chart** menu and **Move Chart**.

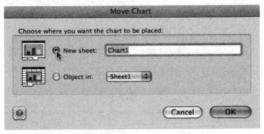

Figure 14-8

18. Your project is now complete!

Plant Community Pie Chart
Activity 15

Objectives

Each student will enter data into a spreadsheet to create a pie chart representing the different types of plants that make up a community within a local ecosystem. He or she will also insert functions within the spreadsheet to automatically express the data as a percentage.

Benchmarks for Technology Standards

Students will know the characteristics, uses, and basic features of computer software programs, including:

- knowing the common features and uses of spreadsheets
- using spreadsheet software to update, add, and delete data, and to produce charts

Learning Objectives

At the end of this lesson, students will be able to:

1. Create a new spreadsheet document.
2. Know the various terms associated with spreadsheets, including *rows*, *columns*, and *cells*.
3. Enter data into a spreadsheet.
4. Adjust the alignment of data within a cell.
5. Change the style of the font within a spreadsheet.
6. Change the format of a number within a cell.
7. Create and format a pie chart from data entered within a spreadsheet.
8. Change the font size of labels within a pie chart.
9. Change the fill color of a pie chart.
10. Apply underline to a chart title.

Before the Computer

This activity can be completed using most versions of Microsoft Excel, Open Office, and iWorks. The procedure for formatting charts using spreadsheets may vary depending on the software and version your school uses. Make sure to try the activity with your school's spreadsheet software, and be prepared to modify the chart procedure accordingly.

Variations

Depending on the age and ability level of your students, you may wish to have students go outside and collect their own data on the type and number of different plants located on or near your school. An example of a completed column chart is shown in Figure 15-1.

Plant Community Pie Chart *(cont.)*
Activity 15

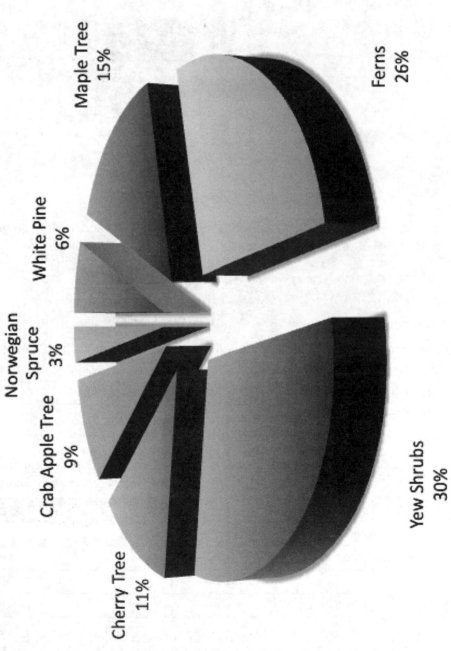

Figure 15-1

Plant Community Pie Chart (cont.)
Activity 15

Procedure

1. Open a new spreadsheet document. Spreadsheets are made up of columns that are identified by letters (A, B, C, etc.) and rows that are identified by numbers (1, 2, 3, etc.).

2. The location within a spreadsheet where a column meets a row is called a cell, and is identified by both a letter and number (Figure 15-2).

Figure 15-2

3. Click into cell **A1**, and type the label "Plant Type." Hit the **tab** key on your keyboard to bring you over to cell **B2**, and type "Amount" (Figure 15-3).

Figure 15-3

4. Next, click and drag over your labels, and use the **Bold** and **Align Center** buttons on your toolbar to center and bold them (Figure 15-4).

Figure 15-4

5. Now you are going to enter your data on the type and number of organisms that make up the plant community in a local ecosystem. Use the table below or your own data to fill in your spreadsheet.

Plant Type	Amount
White Pine	6
Maple Tree	15
Ferns	26
Yew Shrubs	30
Cherry Tree	11
Crab Apple Tree	9
Norwegian Spruce	3

Plant Community Pie Chart *(cont.)*
Activity 15

6. Once you have entered all of your data, highlight both the data and labels, and select the **Insert** menu, and **Chart**.

7. Choose a **3D Exploded Pie** chart (Figure 15-5). Click **Next** twice, and change the title of the chart to "School Plant Community Survey."

Figure 15-5

8. Under **Category Names**, choose **Category Name** and **Percentage**. Click **Next** and in the **Move Chart** window select as **New Sheet**. You can also choose the **Chart** menu and **Move Chart.**

9. Your chart should now be displayed. Sometimes it is necessary to enlarge the size of the font to make text easier to read. To increase the font size of your labels, double-click on one of the labels to bring up the **Format Data Labels** window (Figure 15-6).

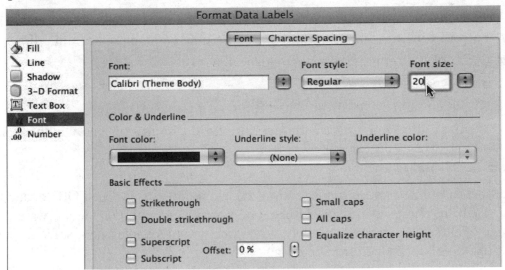

Figure 15-6

10. Click on **Font**, change the font size to **20**, and click **OK**.

11. Next, double-click on the chart's title to bring up the **Format Title** window, and select an **Underline Style** for the title. This will help to separate your title from the pie chart's labels.

12. You can also change the fill color of each of the pie chart's sections by clicking on one section once, and then clicking again to select that particular pie slice to select it. Once it is selected, double-click on it to bring up the **Format Data Series** window. Then you can select a new fill color.

13. Your chart is now complete!

Ice Core Data Dual Line Chart
Activity 16

Objectives

Each student will use data gathered from the Vostok ice core in Antarctica to create a chart that shows the relationship between atmospheric temperature and dust concentration.

Benchmarks for Technology Standards

Students will know the characteristics, uses, and basic features of computer software programs, including:

- knowing the common features and uses of spreadsheets
- using spreadsheet software to update, add, and delete data, and to produce charts

Learning Objectives

At the end of this lesson, students will be able to:

1. Create a new spreadsheet document.
2. Know the various terms associated with spreadsheets, including *rows*, *columns*, and *cells*.
3. Utilize the autofill function to automatically enter a time series into a column of a spreadsheet.
4. Adjust the width of columns within a spreadsheet.
5. Enter data into a spreadsheet.
6. Adjust the alignment and style of the font within a spreadsheet.
7. Create and format a dual line chart with separate axes from data entered within a spreadsheet.

Before the Computer

This activity can be completed using most versions of Microsoft Excel, Open Office, and iWorks. The procedure for formatting charts using spreadsheets may vary depending on the software and version your school uses. Make sure to try the activity with your school's spreadsheet software, and be prepared to modify the chart procedure accordingly.

Variations

Depending on the age and ability level of your students, you may wish to have students create another dual line chart using data on the relationship between carbon dioxide and change in temperature as recorded in the Vostok ice core. An example of a completed dual line chart is shown in Figure 16-1.

Ice Core Data Dual Line Chart (cont.)
Activity 16

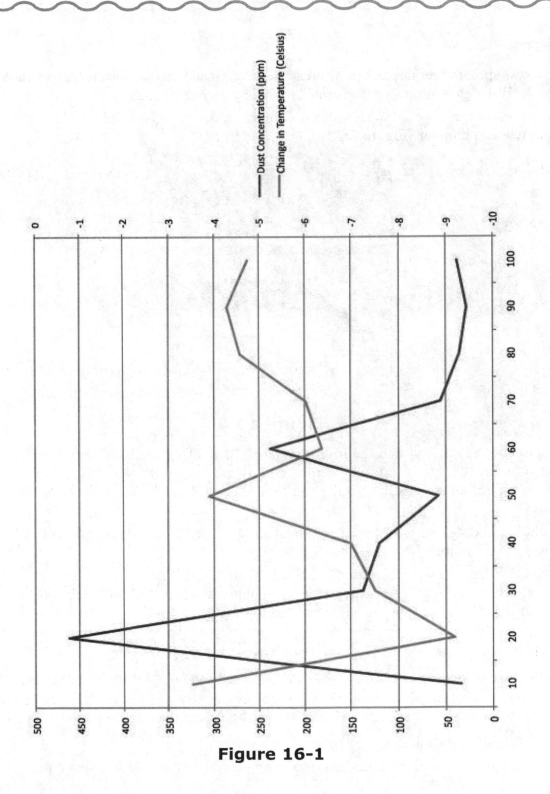

Figure 16-1

Ice Core Data Dual Line Chart *(cont.)*
Activity 16

Procedure

1. Open a new spreadsheet document. Spreadsheets are made up of columns that are identified by letters (A, B, C, etc.) and rows that are identified by numbers (1, 2, 3, etc.).

2. The location within a spreadsheet where a column meets a row is called a cell and is identified by both a letter and number (Figure 16-2).

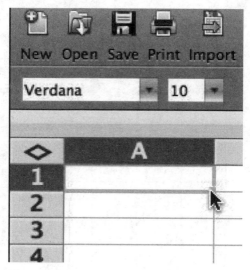

Figure 16-2

3. Click into cell **A1**, and type in the following label: "Age (Thousands of Years Ago)." Hit the **tab** key on your keyboard to bring you over to cell **B1**, and type in the label "Dust Concentration (ppm)." Hit the **tab** key again to bring you over to cell **C1**, and enter "Change in Temperature (Celsius)."

4. Next, click and drag over the three column labels, and use the **Center Alignment** and **Bold** buttons on your toolbar.

5. Now you will have to widen columns A, B, and C so that the labels fit within them. To do this, place your cursor on the line that separates the columns. Then click and drag your cursor to the right until the cell is wide enough for the label to fit (Figure 16-3).

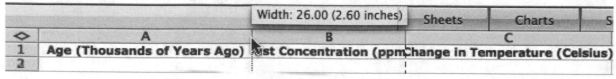

Figure 16-3

6. Next, click into cell **A2** and enter "10."

7. Now hit the **enter** key on your keyboard to bring you down into cell A3, then type "20."

Ice Core Data Dual Line Chart (cont.)
Activity 16

8. Next, you will use the Autofill function to automatically fill in the remaining timescale for your data. To do this, click and drag over only cells **A2** and **A3** (10 and 20) to highlight them. Then move your cursor to the bottom right corner over the little blue dot. Your cursor should then appear as a small plus sign (Figure 16-4).

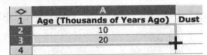

Figure 16-4

9. Once the plus sign appears at the corner of cell **A3**, click and drag down column A until your cursor arrives at cell **A11**. The remaining time data should automatically fill into column A (Figure 16-5).

A	
Age (Thousands of Years Ago)	Dust
10	
20	
30	
40	
50	
60	
70	
80	
90	
100	

Figure 16-5

10. Next, use the data from Table 16-1 below to complete the rest of your spreadsheet. Make sure to enter the minus sign for temperature. (Parts per million [ppm] is a common measurement used in science to measure very small concentrations. For example, 1 ppm of dust in water ice means that there is one particle of dust for every one million water molecules.)

Table 16-1

Age (Thousands of Years Ago)	Dust Concentration (ppm)	Change in Temperature (Celsius)
10	34	-4
20	462	-9
30	137	-8
40	120	-7
50	58	-4
60	238	-6
70	56	-6
80	35	-5
90	27	-4
100	38	-5

Ice Core Data Dual Line Chart *(cont.)*
Activity 16

11. Once you have entered all of your data into your spreadsheet, choose the **Insert** menu, **Chart**, and **Line Chart**.

12. Click **Next**, or choose **Source Data** from the **Chart** menu to bring up the **Select Data Source** window.

13. Select **Age** in the **Series** window, and click on the **Remove** button (Figure 16-6).

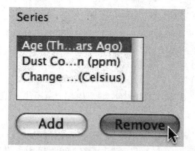

Figure 16-6

14. In the same **Source Data** window, click on the small red arrow icon next to the **Category (x) Axis Labels** box (Figure 16-7).

Figure 16-7

15. Now click and drag over only the numbers in column **A**, and then hit the **enter** key on your keyboard. This will set your x-axis labels in your chart. Hit **OK**.

16. Click **Next** until you get to the **Move Chart** window, and save your chart as a **New Sheet.** Then click **OK**. You can also select the **Chart** menu and **Move Chart** to bring up the **Move Chart** window.

17. Your chart should now appear. Notice that the line representing temperature is very hard to read because its values are much smaller than the dust values. When this is the case, it is best to use separate y-axes for each set of data. To do this, slowly move your cursor over the temperature data line until you see a small box appear (Figure 16-8). Then double-click on it to bring up the **Format Data Series** window.

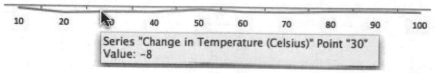

Figure 16-8

18. Click on **Axis**, and choose **Plot Series** on **Secondary Axis**. Then click **OK**.

19. Your temperature data line should now be easier to read.

20. Your project is now complete!

Monthly Temperature Trend Line
Activity 17

Objectives

Each student will use data on long-term temperature to create a line chart. He or she will then insert a trend line to display the statistical trend of the data.

Benchmarks for Technology Standards

Students will know the characteristics, uses, and basic features of computer software programs including:

- Knowing the common features and uses of spreadsheets
- Using spreadsheet software to update, add, and delete data, and to produce charts

Learning Objectives

At the end of this lesson, students will be able to:

1. Create a new spreadsheet document.
2. Know the various terms associated with spreadsheets, including *rows*, *columns*, and *cells*.
3. Utilize the Autofill function to automatically enter dates into a column of a spreadsheet.
4. Adjust the width of columns within a spreadsheet.
5. Enter data into a spreadsheet.
6. Adjust the alignment and style of the font within a spreadsheet.
7. Create and format a line chart from data entered within a spreadsheet.
8. Add a trend line to a chart.

Before the Computer

This activity can be completed using most versions of Microsoft Excel, Open Office, and iWorks. The procedure for formatting charts using spreadsheets may vary depending on the software and version your school uses. Make sure to try the activity with your school's spreadsheet software, and be prepared to modify the chart procedure accordingly.

Variations

Depending on the age and ability level of your students, you may wish to have students gather data from the Internet showing the monthly average temperature for their local area. This type of data can be gathered from the National Weather Service website: **www.weather.gov**. Click on the **Climate** tab, and then click on your state on the map to access climate data for your area. An example of a completed trend line chart is shown in Figure 17-1.

Monthly Temperature Trend Line (cont.)
Activity 17

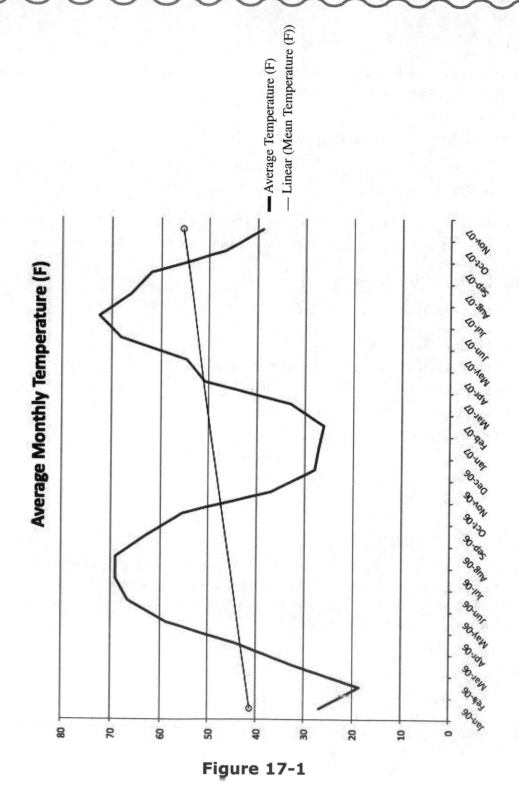

Figure 17-1

Monthly Temperature Trend Line *(cont.)*
Activity 17

Procedure

1. Open a new spreadsheet document. Spreadsheets are made up of columns that are identified by letters (A, B, C, etc.) and rows that are identified by numbers (1, 2, 3, etc.).

2. The location within a spreadsheet where a column meets a row is called a cell and is identified by both a letter and number (Figure 17-2).

Figure 17-2

3. Click into cell **A1**, and type the label "Date." Hit the **tab** key on your keyboard to bring you over to cell **B1**, and type in the label "Average Temperature (F)."

4. Next, click and drag over the two column labels, and use the **Center Alignment** and **Bold** buttons on your toolbar.

5. Now you will have to widen column B so the label fits within it. To do this, take your cursor and place it on the line separating columns B and C. Then click and drag your cursor to the right until the cell is wide enough for the "Average Temperature (F)" label to fit in (Figure 17-3).

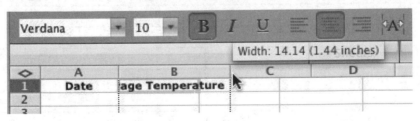

Figure 17-3

6. Next, click into cell **A2** and enter the date "January 2006." Or enter the first date of the data you are using.

7. Now hit the **enter** key on your keyboard to bring you down into cell **A3**, and then type "February 2006."

Monthly Temperature Trend Line *(cont.)*
Activity 17

8. Next, you will use the Autofill function to automatically fill in the remaining dates for your data. To do this, click and drag over only cells **A2** and **A3** to highlight them. Then move your cursor to the bottom right corner over the little blue dot. Your cursor should then appear as a small plus sign (Figure 17-4).

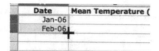

Figure 17-4

9. Once the plus sign appears at the corner of cell **A3**, click and drag down column A until your cursor arrives at cell **A24**. The dates of your temperature record should have automatically filled into column A.

10. Next, use the data from the table below to fill in the rest of your spreadsheet, or use your own climate data.

Date	Average Temperature (F)
Jan-06	27
Feb-06	19
Mar-06	32
Apr-06	44
May-06	59
Jun-06	67
Jul-06	69
Aug-06	69
Sep-06	63
Oct-06	56
Nov-06	37
Dec-06	28
Jan-07	27
Feb-07	26
Mar-07	33
Apr-07	51
May-07	55
Jun-07	68
Jul-07	73
Aug-07	66
Sep-07	62
Oct-07	47
Nov-07	39

Monthly Temperature Trend Line *(cont.)*
Activity 17

11. Once you have entered all of your data into your spreadsheet, choose the **Insert** menu, **Chart**, and **Line Chart**.

12. Click **Next** twice and set the following labels: Chart Title: "Average Monthly Temperature (F)," X-axis: "Date," Y-axis: "Temperature (F)."

13. Click **Next** to bring you to the **Move Chart** window, or select **Move Chart** from the **Chart** menu.

14. Choose **As New Sheet** and click **OK** or **Finish**.

15. Your chart should now be displayed. Now you are going to insert a trend line into your chart. A trend line shows the mathematical trend that your data is showing, and helps to reveal patterns in your data. To insert a trend line, click once on the temperature line on your graph to highlight it (Figure 17-5).

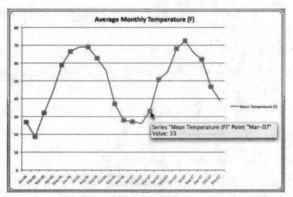

Figure 17-5

16. Once your temperature line has been selected, go to the **Chart** menu and choose **Add Trendline**. This will bring up the **Format Trendline** window.

17. Select **Linear** under trend line type (Figure 17-6).

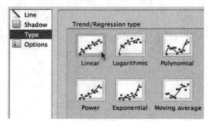

Figure 17-6

18. Click **OK** and a trend line will now appear on your chart showing the trend in average monthly temperature over the time period of your climate data.

19. Your project is now complete!

Water Percent Calculations
Activity 18

Objectives

Each student will utilize a spreadsheet program to create a conversion calculator to convert the volume of water of different categories covering the Earth's surface into percentages.

Benchmarks for Technology Standards

Students will know the characteristics, uses, and basic features of computer software programs including:

- knowing the common features and uses of spreadsheets
- using spreadsheet software to update, add, and delete data, and to produce charts

Learning Objectives

At the end of this lesson, students will be able to:

1. Create a new spreadsheet document.
2. Know the various terms associated with spreadsheets, including *rows*, *columns*, and *cells*.
3. Enter data into a spreadsheet.
4. Adjust the alignment of data within a cell.
5. Enter formulas into a cell and use the sum function.
6. Use cell formulas to calculate data into percentages.
7. Format numbers in a cell to be displayed as a percent.
8. Change the number of decimal places displayed for numbers within a spreadsheet.

Before the Computer

This activity can be completed using most versions of Microsoft Excel, Open Office, and iWorks. Make sure to try the activity with your school's spreadsheet software, and be prepared to modify the procedures accordingly.

Variations

Depending on the age and ability level of your students, you may wish to have students enter other data that they wish to use to calculate percentages. An example of a completed spreadsheet is shown in Figure 18-1.

Water Source	Water Volume (Cubic Miles)	Percent of Total Water
Oceans	321,000,000	96.54%
Glacial Ice	5,844,970	1.76%
Groundwater	5,614,000	1.69%
Lakes, Rivers, Swamps	45,581	0.01%
Total	332,504,551	

Figure 18-1

Water Percent Calculations *(cont.)*
Activity 18

Procedure

1. Open a new spreadsheet document. Spreadsheets are made up of columns that are identified by letters (A, B, C, etc.) and rows that are identified by numbers (1, 2, 3, etc.).

2. The location within a spreadsheet where a column meets a row is called a cell and is identified by both a letter and number (Figure 18-2).

Figure 18-2

3. Click into cell **A1**, and type the label "Water Source."

4. Hit the **tab** key on your keyboard to bring you to cell **B1**, and type "Water Volume (Cubic Miles)."

5. Hit the **tab** key again to bring you into cell **C1**, and type "Percent of Total Water."

6. Click and drag over all of the labels in row 1 to highlight them, and then use the **Bold** and **Align Center** buttons on your tool bar to make the labels bold and centered in each cell (Figure 18-3).

Figure 18-3

7. You will now have to widen your columns B and C so the label fits within them. To do this, take your cursor and move it to the line in between columns B and C, and then click and drag to widen the column so your label fits (Figure 18-4). Repeat for column C.

◇	A	B	C	D
			Width: 23.43 (2.35 inches)	
1	**Water Source**	**Water Volume (Cubic Miles)**	**Percent of Total Water**	
2				

Figure 18-4

8. Next, fill in the data about the type and volume of water on the Earth using the data table below.

Water Source	Water Volume (Cubic Miles)
Oceans	321,000,000
Glacial Ice	5,844,970
Groundwater	5,614,000
Lakes, Rivers, Swamps	45,581

Water Percent Calculations *(cont.)*
Activity 18

9. Once your data is entered, you will have to widen column A so all the water sources are readable.

10. Next, click into cell **A6** and type "Total." Then, click into cell **B6**.

11. Now you are going to enter a formula into cell B6 that will automatically calculate the total amount of water on the Earth in cubic miles. To do this, choose the **Insert** menu, and select **Function**.

12. In the **Insert Function** window, double click on **SUM** (Figure 18-5).

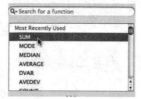

Figure 18-5

13. Now you will select the cells that you wish to add together within your sum function. To do this, click and drag your cursor over the numbers in cells **B2** to **B5**. This should automatically insert them into the **Function Arguments** window. Click **OK**.

14. The sum function should now be set up within cell B6. Now hit the **enter** key on your keyboard, and the total water volume should be displayed as **332,504,551**.

15. Next you are going to use a function to calculate the percentage that each type of water occupies on the Earth. Click into cell **C2**, and enter the following formula: **=B2/B6**. This formula takes the value from cell B2 and divides it by the value within cell B6.

16. Hit the **enter** key on your keyboard to bring you down to cell **C3** and type the formula **=B3/B6** in order to divide cell B3 by B6, then hit **enter** on your keyboard.

17. Repeat this same process for the remaining data in cells B4 and B5.

18. Next, you will need to format the numbers in column C so they are rounded to one decimal place and will also be displayed as a percentage. To do this, click and drag over the numbers in column C to highlight them.

19. Go to the **Format** menu and select **Cells**. In the **Format Cells** window, click on **Number**, then change the decimal places to **2**, and click **OK**. Your numbers in column C should now be rounded to the nearest hundredth (Figure 18-6).

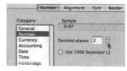

Figure 18-6

20. Next, with the same cells still highlighted, return to the **Format Cells** window and click on **Percentage** under the **Category** list, then click **OK**. Your cells should now be displayed as percentages.

21. Your project is now complete!

Technology Expenditures *(cont.)*
Activity 19

Objectives

Each student will utilize a spreadsheet program to create a spreadsheet of technology expenditures.

Benchmarks for Technology Standards

Students will know the characteristics, uses, and basic features of computer software programs including:

- knowing the common features and uses of spreadsheets
- using spreadsheet software to update, add, and delete data, and to produce charts

Learning Objectives

At the end of this lesson, students will be able to:

1. Create a new spreadsheet document.
2. Know the various terms associated with spreadsheets, including *rows*, *columns*, and *cells*.
3. Enter data into a spreadsheet.
4. Adjust the alignment of data within a cell.
5. Enter formulas into a cell.
6. Format numbers in a cell to be displayed as a currency.
7. Insert a header into a spreadsheet.

Before the Computer

This activity can be completed using most versions of Microsoft Excel, Open Office, and iWorks. Make sure to try the activity with your school's spreadsheet software, and be prepared to modify the procedures accordingly.

Variations

Depending on the age and ability level of your students, instead of using the example technology expenditures provided, you may wish to have students create their own budget worksheet using different data. An example of a completed spreadsheet is shown in Figure 19-1.

Technology Budget 2009-10			
Hardware Budget	$15,000.00	Software Budget	$10,000.00
Expenditures		Expenditures	
10 - 4 GB Flash Drives	$106.89	School Tool	$5,789.12
5 - Dell Inspiron Computers	$3,350.00	Internet Filtering	$3,443.00
10 - HP Printers	$890.00		
Hardware Balance	$10,653.11	Software Balance	$767.88
Total Technology Balance	$11,420.99		

Figure 19-1

Technology Expenditures (cont.)
Activity 19

Procedure

1. Open a new spreadsheet document. Spreadsheets are made up of columns that are identified by letters (A, B, C, etc.) and rows that are identified by numbers (1, 2, 3, etc.).

2. The location within a spreadsheet where a column meets a row is called a cell and is identified by both a letter and number (Figure 19-2).

Figure 19-2

3. Click into cell **A1**, and type the label "Technology Budget 2009-10." Increase the font size to **12**, and use the **Bold** button to make this label bold.

4. You will now have to widen your column **A** so the label fits within the cell. To do this, take your cursor and move it to the line in between columns A and B, and then click and drag to widen the column so your label fits (Figure 19-3).

Figure 19-3

5. Next, click into cell **A3** and type "Hardware Budget." Hit the **tab** key, enter the following into cell **B3**: "15,000," and hit **enter** on your keyboard.

6. Now click into cell **A4** and type: "Expenditures:." Make the Hardware Budget and Expenditures cells bold. Hit the **enter** key on your keyboard to bring you down to cell **A5** and type "10 - 4 GB Flash Drives." Hit the **tab** key, and enter "106.89" in cell **B5**. Click into cell **A6** and type "5 - Dell Inspiron Computers," then hit the tab key to move you into cell **B6**. In this cell, enter "3,350."

7. Next click into cell **A7** and type "10 - HP printers." Hit the **tab** and enter "890."

8. Click into cell **A12** and type "Hardware Balance." Make the title in this cell bold.

9. Now you are going to enter a formula into cell B12 that will display the balance of the hardware budget minus the three expenditures. Click into cell **B12** and enter the following formula: **=B3-B5-B6-B7**. Hit **enter** on your keyboard, and the balance of your hardware budget will be automatically displayed as "10,653." Also make this cell bold.

Technology Expenditures (cont.)
Activity 19

10. Next you will change the format of the numbers in your hardware balance so they appear as currency. To do this, click and drag over all of the numbers in column **B** to highlight them, go to the **Format** menu, and choose **Cells**. Click on **Currency** in the **Category** list. Make sure the **Decimal Places** are set to **2**, and the **Currency** symbol to **$** (Figure 19-4). Click **OK**.

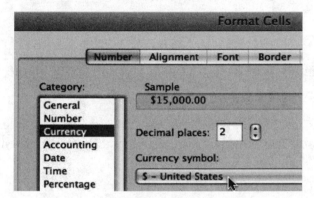

Figure 19-4

11. Your budget should now be displayed as currency.

12. Next, click into cell **C3** and type in the following: "Software Budget." Hit the **tab** key, and enter the following into cell **D3**: "10,000." Hit **enter** on your keyboard.

13. Now click into cell **C4** and type "Expenditures:." Make the "Software Budget" and "Expenditures" cells bold. You may also have to widen column C to make the labels readable. Hit the **enter** key on your keyboard to bring you down to cell **C5** and type: "School Tool." Hit the **tab** key, and enter "5789.12" in cell **D5**. Click into cell **C6** and type "Internet Filtering," then hit the **tab** key to move you into cell **D6**. In this cell enter "3,443."

14. Click into cell **C12** and type "Software Balance." Make the title in this cell bold.

15. Now you are going to enter a formula into cell D12 that will display the balance of the Software Budget minus the two expenditures. Click into cell **D12** and enter the following formula: **=D3-D5-D6**. Hit **enter** on your keyboard, and the balance of your Software Budget will be automatically displayed as "768." Also, make this cell bold.

16. Format the numbers in column D to display as currency the same way as you did for column B.

17. Next, click into cell **A14**. In this cell you are going to type "Total Technology Balance." Make this title bold and adjust the column width if necessary. Click into cell **B14** and enter the following formula: **=B12+D12**. This will add the sum of cells **B12** and **D12**, which will represent the total balance for your budget.

18. Hit the **enter** key on your keyboard. Format cell B14 as currency like the other cells.

19. Finally, click into cell **B14** and choose the **Format** menu and **Cells**. Click the **Font** button and change the color to **red**. Click **OK**.

20. Your project is now complete!

Internet Safety Tutorial
Activity 20

Objectives

Each student will become familiar with how to use presentation software to create a simple presentation.

Benchmarks for Technology Standards

Students will know the characteristics, uses, and basic features of computer software programs, including:

knowing the common features and uses of desktop publishing software (e.g., documents are created, designed, and formatted for publication; data, and graphics can be imported into a document using desktop software)

Learning Objectives

At the end of this lesson, students will be able to:

1. Create a new presentation document.
2. Know the various terms associated with presentations including *slides*, *theme*, *slide show*, *normal view*, *title*, and *subtitle*.
3. Select a theme for a presentation.
4. Insert a title into a presentation.
5. Insert a subtitle into a presentation.
6. Insert an image into a presentation.
7. Change the size of the font within a presentation.
8. Add an effect to text within a presentation.
9. Create a new slide within a presentation.
10. Create a transition within a presentation.
11. View the presentation as a slide show.

Before the Computer

This activity can be completed using most presentation software including PowerPoint, Open Office, and Keynote.

Variations

Depending on the age and ability level of your students, you may wish to have students create a more detailed presentation on Internet safety.

Internet Safety Tutorial *(cont.)*
Activity 20

Procedure

1. Begin this activity by opening a new presentation. In this activity, you will create a slide show about Internet safety.

2. First you will choose a theme for your presentation. A theme is a specific set of colors and font styles for your presentation. Go to the **Format** menu, select **Theme** to bring up the theme gallery (Figure 20-1). Choose a theme that you like.

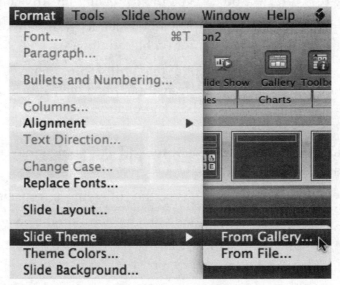

Figure 20-1

3. The first slide will appear. Click into the text box that reads **Click to Add Title**. Type in the following title: "Internet Safety."

4. In the **Click to Add Subtitles** box, type "by (your name)."

5. Next you are going to apply an effect to your title. Choose the **Slide Show** menu and select **Custom Animation**. In the **Custom Animation** window, click the **Add Emphasis Effect** button next to **Add Effect** (Figure 20-2).

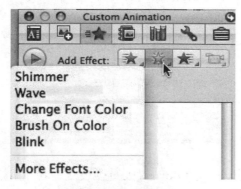

Figure 20-2

Internet Safety Tutorial *(cont.)*
Activity 20

6. Select one of the effects you like. To see how it works after you select it, click the **Play** button just to the right of **Add Effect**. To remove an effect, right-click (or control-click) on it in the **Custom Animation** window and choose **Delete**.

7. Next, go to the **Insert** Menu and choose **New Slide**. This will insert a new slide into your presentation. Click into the **Click to Add Title** box and type "Internet Safety Tip #1."

8. Apply another custom animation to this title.

9. Next, click into **Click to Add Text** box. Type the following information:

"Remember never to give out personal information, such as your name, home address, school name, or telephone number in a chat room or on bulletin boards."

10. Now you are going to insert a transition effect that will occur when you go from slide 1 to slide 2 during your slide show. To insert a transition, open the **Slide Show** menu and choose **Transitions**. Select a transition that you like, and change the speed to **Slow** under **Modify Transitions or Options**.

11. Insert another new slide. Click into the **Click to Add Title** box and type "Internet Safety Tip #2." Add another custom animation to the title.

12. Next, click in the **Click to Add Text** box. Type the following information:

"Never send a picture of yourself to someone you chat with on the computer without a parent's permission."

13. Choose a new transition for this slide.

14. Continue to add more slides, animations, and transitions using the following information:

"Tip #3: Never write to someone who has made you feel uncomfortable or scared."

"Tip #4: Do not meet someone or have them visit you without the permission of your parents."

"Tip #5: Tell your parents right away if you read anything on the Internet that makes you feel uncomfortable."

"Tip #6: Remember that people online may not be who they say they are. Someone who says that she is a 12-year-old girl could really be an older man."

15. Finally, insert a final slide that reads: "THE END."

16. Your presentation is now complete! To view it as a slide show, click on the title slide in the **slide sort** window. Then click on the **Slide Show** button (Figure 20-3). Click your mouse to advance to your next slide.

Figure 20-3